The Fearful Rise of Markets

Vice President, Publisher: Tim Moore
Associate Publisher and Director of Marketing: Amy Neidlinger
Executive Editor: Jim Boyd
Editorial Assistant: Pamela Boland
Operations Manager: Gina Kanouse
Senior Marketing Manager: Julie Phifer
Publicity Manager: Laura Czaja
Assistant Marketing Manager: Megan Colvin
Cover Designer: Alan Clements
Managing Editor: Kristy Hart
Project Editors: Jovana San Nicolas-Shirley, Lori Lyons
Copy Editor: Julie Anderson
Proofreader: Apostrophe Editing Services
Indexer: Erika Millen
Compositor: Jake McFarland
Manufacturing Buyer: Dan Uhrig

© 2010 by John Authers

Publishing as FT Press

Upper Saddle River, New Jersey 07458

FT Press offers excellent discounts on this book when ordered in quantity for bulk purchases or special sales. For more information, please contact U.S. Corporate and Government Sales, 1-800-382-3419, corpsales@pearsontechgroup.com. For sales outside the U.S., please contact International Sales at international@pearson.com.

Company and product names mentioned herein are the trademarks or registered trademarks of their respective owners.

Printed in the United States of America

Second Printing December 2010

ISBN-10: 0-13-707299-6
ISBN-13: 978-0-13-707299-6

Pearson Education LTD.
Pearson Education Australia PTY, Limited.
Pearson Education Singapore, Pte. Ltd.
Pearson Education North Asia, Ltd.
Pearson Education Canada, Ltd.
Pearson Educación de Mexico, S.A. de C.V.
Pearson Education—Japan
Pearson Education Malaysia, Pte. Ltd.

Library of Congress Cataloging-in-Publication Data
Authers, John, 1966-
  The fearful rise of markets: global bubbles, synchronized meltdowns, and how to prevent them in the future / John Authers.
    p. cm.
  ISBN-13: 978-0-13-707299-6 (hardback : alk. paper)
  ISBN-10: 0-13-707299-6 (hardback : alk. paper) 1. International economic integration. 2. Globalization—Economic aspects. 3. Financial crises. 4. Economic stabilization. I. Title.
HF1418.5.A98 2010
  338.5'42—dc22
                                    2010001943

For Andie, Josie, and Jamie

Contents

Acknowledgments

I submitted the manuscript for this book on the twentieth anniversary of my first day at the *Financial Times*, so I must first acknowledge my debt to the news organization where I have spent all my working life. I learned substantially all that I know about the world of investment during my career at the *Financial Times*, which has involved living in three countries, traveling to many more, and reporting on many of the events in this book.

I learned much from all the many colleagues with whom I have worked, and I am grateful to all of them. I thank Lionel Barber, Martin Dickson, and Daniel Bogler for allowing me the time off needed to finish this book. Keith Fray, the *Financial Times* deputy head of statistics who suffers daily demands from me for graphics and information at the best of times, checked all the graphics. In particular, I want to thank Philip Coggan, my mentor and predecessor, who probably helped me more than anyone else at the paper, and my current colleague in New York, Michael Mackenzie, who might know more about markets than anyone else I know.

My studies at Columbia Business School, where I received an MBA in 2000, were also formative. I want to thank all my professors there, but in particular David Beim, Joel Brockner, Franklin Edwards, Paul Glasserman, and Bruce Greenwald for the many lessons I learned that proved invaluable for writing this book. It is also appropriate to thank the Knight-Bagehot Fellowship and George A. Wiegers, for providing me with the funding for the MBA.

This book is the result of my own conclusions, but these were formed by talking to a lot of people. In particular, I want to thank the following for interviews that helped in preparing the book: Antoine van Agtmael, Robert Arnott, Robert Barbera, David Beim, Mohamed

El-Erian, Gary Gorton, Robert Jaeger, Tim Lee, Jamie Lee, Andrew Lo, George Magnus, Benoit Mandelbrot, Rick di Mascio, Michael Mauboussin, James Melcher, Amin Rajan, Jeremy Siegel, Philip Verleger, and Dimitri Vayanos.

Others have provided me with regular inputs of their research and have been invaluable in guiding me through the investment maze. In particular, I want to thank David Bowers, Ian Harnett, Chis Watling, Tim Bond, Vinny Catalano, Alan Ruskin, Marc Chandler, Simon Derrick, Mansoor Mohi-Uddin, Albert Edwards, Jeremy Grantham, Elroy Dimson, Mark Lapolla, Tobias Levkovich, James Montier, Russell Napier, James Paulsen, David Ranson, Alan Rohrbach, Joseph Stiglitz, Richard Thaler, and the entire staff of London's Capital Economics and Lombard Street Research.

This is a work of journalism, not an academic book, but the usual academic disclaimer applies. The merits are thanks to these people; the mistakes are all mine.

I relied on my own reporting, and on that of my *Financial Times* colleagues wherever possible. Details of the original articles appear in the Notes. I also read many books, which appear in the Bibliography.

At Pearson Education, I want to thank Chris Cudmore, Jim Boyd, and Russ Hall, who challenged me to take the book into different but better directions. Thanks also to Jovana Shirley and Lori Lyons for the finishing touches during production.

Robert Jaeger, Jennifer Hughes, Anora Mahmudova, and Paul Griffin all kindly read early drafts and gave me comments. My father, David Authers, read possibly every draft I produced and continues to be my most perceptive critic. The staff of Fort Washington Public Library provided a pleasant working environment for me.

Finally, and most important, I want to thank my wife, Sara Silver, for encouraging me while I finished this book, at a point when she had only just herself gone through the much more arduous process of giving birth to our third child, as well as for her ever exacting and invaluable editing; and my children Andie, Josie, and Jamie for giving me just enough peace to get it written and enough moments of joy to remind me that there are far more important things in life than finance.

About the Author

John Authers, as investment editor for the *Financial Times*, served for several years as its main commentator on international markets. In this role, he became one of the world's most influential financial journalists, writing its influential Short View and Long View columns five days each week. As this book went to press, he took over as the head of the *Financial Times'* flagship Lex column.

During a 20-year career with the paper, based in London, New York, and Mexico City, Authers has won many awards, particularly for his work on investment and for his coverage of the credit crisis. This is his second book. He lives in New York, with his wife Sara Silver, also a financial journalist, and their three children.

Foreword

I suspect that most of us have a daily routine when it comes to reading the news and looking for insightful commentary and analysis. I know that I do; and my routine includes seeing what John Authers has to say.

John's daily column in the *Financial Times* is a "must read" for many of us who are not just interested in markets, but also involved in their inner workings, daily fluctuations, and volatile emotions. His writings provide us with timely insights into market developments and the outlook; and they fuel interesting, and at times, lively debates in the marketplace.

You will understand, therefore, how delighted and honored I was when John asked me to write a foreword for this wonderful book. I also felt intimidated at the thought of appearing in print together with one of the best writers in the financial media. Thankfully, this foreword is of a length that would limit any meaningful comparison of my approach to writing with John's engaging and insightful style.

This enjoyable and fast-moving book is written in the style of John's daily columns—concise, relevant, and containing perceptive examples. Think of the book as your vehicle for a journey of discovery. Each stop will precisely inform you of the forces that have come together to determine market valuations and correlations—or, in the words of John, the drivers of the rise in markets, their collapse, and their ongoing re-emergence (albeit one still vulnerable to failures and weak regulatory and private infrastructure).

During this journey, you will discover why markets can move together for a long time and to an excessive degree (for example, the formation of "bubbles") before correlations collapse in a spectacular and wrenching fashion; why so many investment managers fall victim to herd behavior; why inappropriately specified and monitored principal/agent relationships result in a misalignment of incentives between the end investors and the managers that work for them; how risk management techniques can morph from being mitigators of risk to amplifiers; and why regulators have so much trouble maintaining their finger on the pulse of the markets.

As you proceed with your journey, you will come across a lot of interesting tidbits, including how emerging markets acquired the name and evolved into an investible asset class. Most importantly in my eyes, you will also see how society is being forced today into important tradeoffs between stability and efficiency—and yet this imperative balance (that will impact both current and future generations) is being inadequately considered by governments around the world.

The timing of this book is also highly appropriate. It is published at a time when, having survived a near-death experience during the 2008-09 global financial crisis, too many market participants have reverted to old and eventually unsustainable mindsets and behaviors; at a time when regulators are slipping in both the design and implementation of measures to strengthen market infrastructure and limit systemic risk; and at a time when political expediency risks overwhelming economic and financial logic.

Yes, this book is about a highly relevant journey and about great timing. It is also about what the destination is *likely* to be, as well as what it *should* be.

On reading the book, I suspect that you will come away with a much clearer understanding of the remaining potential for market accidents and policy mistakes. You will be exposed to a summary of what governments need to do to lower the risk of additional large market disruptions. And you will be armed with an expanded toolset to consider where risks and opportunities lay in today's (and tomorrow's) marketplace.

This book is of even greater relevance if you buy into the work that my PIMCO colleagues and I have done on the manner in which markets and economies will likely reset after the 2008-09 global financial crisis. Our work suggests that rather than be subject to a conventional reversion to the most recent mean (the "old normal"), the global system is now engaged on a bumpy, multi-year journey to a "new normal."

For reasons cited in John's book—including inadequate framing, herding behavior, and backward-looking internal commitments and principal/agent problems—it will take time for societies to fully recognize and adapt to the regime changes. This is not for lack of evidence. After all, who would deny the multi-year influence of the sudden, simultaneous, and large deterioration in the public finances of advanced economies; the unexpected surge in several of these economies' unemployment rates, coupled with the realization that the rates will stay high for an unusually long time; the consequential erosion in the institutional standing of both private and public entities; and the growing importance of socio-political factors in driving economies and markets?

My bottom line is a simple one: John's book should be read by all those interested in the way markets operate, be they investors, analysts, or policy makers. Yes, markets are here to stay; and, yes, they are still the best construct for organizing, valuing, and allocating resources. But this should not blind us to the fact that markets do occasionally fail.

Markets do become overly synchronized at times and overshoot, and they can involve activities that are insufficiently understood and inadequately supported by the necessary infrastructure. By neatly and succinctly speaking to all this, John Authers' book also gives us hope that markets could also be made to work better in enhancing global welfare.

Mohamed A. El-Erian, CEO and co-CIO of PIMCO, and author of *When Markets Collide*

The Fearful Rise of Markets: A Timeline

The Rise

November 23, 1954: U.S. stock market recovers from the Great Crash

Strict post-Depression regulation of U.S. finance is in place: Commercial banks are covered by deposit insurance and barred from investment banking. Fixed exchange rates are linked to gold under Bretton Woods. Banks dominate finance. Investment is dominated by individuals investing their own money. The young world is in the post-war Baby Boom, while the capitalist world is divided from the Third World and the Communist Bloc. Mainstream investors have no access to investing in commodities, foreign exchange, credit default risk, or emerging markets. All these factors change in the next half century, creating the conditions for unrelated markets to overheat and crash together in a synchronized bubble.

1962: Launch of Fidelity's Magellan Fund

Investment managers like Fidelity start publicizing their returns and launching big new funds. The industry is driven by the aim to accumulate assets. Ranking organizations start publishing league tables comparing funds' short-term performance. Markets are now driven by people using other people's money; their pay and their benchmarks encourage them to herd together.

1969: Launch of the first Money Market Fund

Capital markets strip banks of many core functions. Money market mutual funds even offer checkbooks. This gets around strict 1930s restrictions to avert bank runs but creates apparent bank deposits that do not have deposit insurance; it takes lending decisions from banks' lending officers and gives them to markets; and it forces banks to look for new, often riskier lines of business.

1971: Gold standard ends

Nixon exits the gold standard; a necessary condition for bubbles. With gold no longer the anchor, currencies depend on central banks. If they lose their credibility, the anchor of the world economy is now the price of oil, not gold.

1975: First index fund launched

Index funds create benchmarks for managers to crowd around and make the market more prone to bubbles as they take a growing share of assets.

1982: Launch of the first Emerging Markets Fund

The World Bank rebrands Lesser Developed Countries as "Emerging Markets," and sets up funds to buy shares on their stock markets, opening them as a new asset class to mainstream investors for the first time. Once uncorrelated with developed world stocks, they start to synchronize with them when the same investors hold both, and the creation of emerging market indexes helps create a "herding" effect in emerging markets.

1984: Reform of mortgage-backed bonds

Ronald Reagan allows investment banks to trade bonds that are backed by big pools of mortgages and makes it easier for investors to buy them. This increases the power of Fannie Mae and Freddie Mac and eases the problems for struggling small U.S. banks. It also means the agents who decide to extend loans are not on the hook if the mortgage defaults—and that investors in other markets could trade in and out of mortgage debt—helping to inflate the synchronized bubble.

January 1990: Crash of Japan leads to the yen carry trade

A carry trade creates cheap money by borrowing in a currency with low interest rates, putting money into currencies with high interest rates and pocketing the difference. When Japan's bubble bursts in 1990, low rates in yen create a carry trade. Equity investors finance themselves this way—so the yen starts to move in line with stocks.

September 1992: Sterling's Black Monday spurs foreign exchange as an asset class

Big coups for currency investors in the early 1990s prompt interest in forex as its own asset class. Big investors set up funds just to make bets on exchange rates.

December 1996: Alan Greenspan warns against irrational exuberance

Aging baby boomers' confidence, and their need to save for retirement, drive huge flows of money into mutual funds. That inflates the stock market and further pushes fund managers to crowd into hot stocks. They become the world's investor of last resort.

1997: Asia crisis prompts Asian countries to build up reserves of dollars

Asian countries suffer a series of devaluations, come close to default, and then suffer years of austerity. This prompts China and other Asian countries to build stockpiles of dollars—making U.S. interest rates lower, pumping more money into markets.

March 1998: Citigroup and Bank of America mergers create banks that are "too big to fail"

Global mega-mergers leave many banks so big and important to the economy that they know governments cannot let them fail, creating moral hazard—and incentives to take risks. Banks go global with operations around the world, increasing global correlations.

August 1998: Long-Term Capital Management melts down

Long-Term Capital Management, the biggest hedge fund at the time, sparks an international seizure for credit markets—an early warning of a super-bubble. It is rescued and the Fed cuts rates, inflating a bubble in tech stocks and stoking moral hazard.

2000: Dot-com bubble bursts

Technology stocks crash after forming history's biggest stock market bubble—the culmination of irrational exuberance, decades of herd-like behavior, and the recent injection of cheap money and moral hazard by the Federal Reserve. The Fed responds by cutting rates, prompting an early rebound for stock markets, the rise of hedge funds, and bubbles in credit and housing.

2001: Emerging markets rebranded BRICs

Goldman Sachs predicts great growth for the BRICs (Brazil, Russia, India, and China) and ignites a new emerging markets boom. The flows of money tied the BRICs to other stock markets and pushed up commodity prices and emerging market exchange rates.

2004: Commodities become an asset class

Big investing institutions pour into commodity futures after academic research shows they offer strong returns uncorrelated to the stock market. The new money helps make commodities correlate far more with stocks. Rising commodity prices also push up emerging markets and exchange rates.

2005: Default risk becomes an asset class

Credit derivatives open the world of credit and loans to mainstream investors. Credit starts to correlate closely with equities, bonds, and commodities and drives the rise in U.S. house prices and the subprime mortgage boom. By creating cheap leverage, the credit boom inflates bubbles simultaneously across the world.

The Fall

February 27, 2007: Shanghai Surprise ends the Great Moderation

The bubble rests on the extreme low volatility and low interest rates of 2003–2006. Volatility suddenly rises, making financial engineering much harder.

June 7, 2007: Ten-year Treasury yields hit 5.05 percent

Investors sell bonds, pushing up their yields and breaking a downward trend that had lasted two decades—this changes the mathematics for all credit products.

June 19, 2007: Bear Stearns Hedge Fund appeals for help

The hedge funds' lenders take possession of subprime-backed securities and auction them, revealing confusion over how much they are worth.

August 3, 2007: Pundit Jim Cramer declares "Armageddon" in the credit markets

U.S. retail investors discover that U.S. banks have stopped lending to each other.

August 7–9, 2007: Big quantitative hedge funds suffer unprecedented losses

One equity hedge fund liquidating its trades in the wake of the Bear Stearns incident leads to unprecedented losses for a group of big hedge funds that supposedly have no exposure to the market.

August 9, 2007: European Central Bank intervenes after BNP Paribas money funds close

This is "The Day the World Changed" according to Northern Rock—money markets panic intensifies on both sides of the Atlantic.

August 17, 2007: Fed cuts rates after Countrywide funding crisis

The biggest U.S. mortgage lender teeters on the brink of bankruptcy; then the Fed cuts rates—prompting new waves of money into emerging markets and rebounds in the U.S. and Europe.

September 13, 2007: The run on Northern Rock

UK bank customers queue up to remove their deposits, damaging confidence in the UK.

October 31, 2007: World stock markets peak

Fears of losses at Citigroup prompt a sell-off on November 1.

March 16, 2008: Bear Stearns rescued by JP Morgan

Bear Stearns falls victim to a "bank run"—the U.S. government helps JP Morgan to buy it, stoking the belief that bailouts will be available and pushing up commodity markets.

July 14, 2008: Oil peaks and the dollar rebounds—the end of the "decoupling trade"

The 2008 oil spike ends, ending an inflation scare. Oil, foreign exchange, and stock markets simultaneously reverse, creating big losses and forcing investors to repay debts.

September 7, 2008: Fannie Mae and Freddie Mac nationalized

Preferred shareholders take losses, shocking markets and prompting a run on all financial institutions seen as vulnerable.

September 15, 2008: Lehman Brothers bankrupt

Negotiations to sell it fail; Merrill Lynch sells to Bank of America; AIG appeals for help.

September 18, 2008: AIG rescued; Reserve Fund breaks the buck; money market panics

A money market fund "breaks the buck" because it holds Lehman bonds, leading to panic withdrawals from money funds; AIG requires an $85 billion rescue, prompting fears for European banks it insured.

September 29, 2008: Congress votes down the TARP bailout package.

Confidence in political institutions collapses. Confusion in European Union over how to coordinate protecting bank deposits makes this all the worse.

October 6–10, 2008: Global correlated crash

Virtually all the world's stock markets drop by one-fifth in one week—the unprecedented fall across all asset classes demonstrates that there had been a synchronized bubble.

The Fearful Rise

October 24, 2008: Emerging markets hit bottom as China rolls out stimulus plan

China's aggressive expansion of lending and the Fed's supply of dollars to emerging market central banks avert an all-out emerging market default crisis.

March 9, 2009: Bank stocks, and developed markets in general, hit bottom and rally

A rally starts after Citigroup says it is trading profitably. Confidence returns that big banks can avoid nationalization.

Chapter 1

The Fearful Rise of Markets

"A rising market can still bring the reality of riches. This, in turn, can draw more and more people to participate.... The government preventatives and controls are ready. In the hands of a determined government, their efficacy cannot be doubted. There are, however, a hundred reasons why a government will determine not to use them."[1]

J.K. Galbraith, 1954

World markets are synchronized, and far more prone to bubbles and meltdowns than they used to be. Why?

It was in March 2007 that I realized that the world's markets had each other in a tight and deadly embrace. A week earlier, global stock markets had suffered the "Shanghai Surprise," when a 9 percent fall on the Shanghai stock exchange led to a day of turmoil across the world. By that afternoon on Wall Street, the Dow Jones Industrial Average suddenly dropped by 2 percent in a matter of seconds. A long era of unnatural calm for markets was over.

Watching from the *Financial Times'* New York newsroom, I was trying to make sense of it. Stocks were rising again after the shock, but people were jittery. Currency markets were in upheaval.

I anxiously checked the Bloomberg terminal. One screen showed minute-by-minute action that day in the S&P 500, the main index of the U.S. stock market. Then I called up a minute-by-minute chart of the exchange rate of the Japanese yen against the U.S. dollar. At first I thought I had mistyped. The chart was identical to the S&P.

If it were not so sinister, it might have been funny. As the day wore on and turned into the next, we in the newsroom watched the two charts snaking identical courses across the screen. Every time the S&P rose, the dollar rose against the yen and vice versa. What on earth was going on?

Correlations like this were unnatural. In the years leading up to the Shanghai Surprise, the yen and the S&P had moved completely independently. They are two of the most liquid markets on earth, traded historically by completely different people, and there are many unconnected reasons why people would exchange in and out of the yen (for trade or tourism), or buy or sell a U.S. stock (thanks to the latest news from companies in Corporate America). But since the Shanghai Surprise, statisticians show that any move in the S&P is sufficient to explain 40 percent of moves in the yen, and vice versa. As they should have nothing in common, this implies that neither market is being priced efficiently. Instead, these entangled markets are driven by the same investors, using the same flood of speculative money.

The issue is vital because as I write (in early 2010), markets are even more tightly linked than they were in early 2007. It is once again impossible to tell the difference between charts of the dollar and of the U.S. stock market. Links with the prices of commodities and credit remain perversely tight.

The Shanghai Surprise, we now know, marked the start of the worst global financial crisis for at least 80 years, and plunged the global economy into freefall in 2009—the most truly global economic crash on record.

Inefficiently priced markets drove this dreadful process. If currencies are buoyed or depressed by speculation, they skew the terms of global trade. Governments' control over their own economies is compromised if exchange rates make their goods too cheap or too expensive. An excessive oil price can drive the world into recession. Extreme food prices mean starvation for billions. Money pouring into emerging markets stokes inflation and destabilizes the economies on which the world now relies for its growth. If credit becomes too cheap and then too expensive for borrowers, then an unsustainable boom is followed by a bust. And for investors, risk management becomes impossible when all markets move in unison. With nowhere to hide, everyone's pension plan takes a hit if markets crash together. In one week of October 2008, the value of global retirement assets took a hit of about 20 percent.

Such a cataclysm should have shaken out the speculation from the system for a generation, but evidently it has not—and this implies that the risk of another synchronized collapse is very much alive.

What I hope to do in this short book is to explain how the world's markets became synchronized, how they formed a bubble, how they all managed to crash together and then rebound together, and what can be done to prevent another synchronized bust in the future. In the process, I also hope to provide some guidelines for investors trying to deal with this situation.

Investment bubbles inevitably recur from time to time because they are rooted in human psychology. Markets are driven by the interplay of greed and fear. When greed swamps fear, as it tends to do at least once in every generation, an irrational bubble will result. When the pendulum snaps back to fear, the bubble bursts, causing a crash.

History provides examples at least as far back as the seventeenth century "Tulip Mania," in which wealthy Dutch merchants paid their life savings for one tulip bulb. Then came the South Sea Bubble in England and the related Mississippi Bubble in France, as investors fell over themselves to finance prospecting in the New World. Later there were bubbles in canals. The Victorian era saw a bubble in U.S. railroad stocks; the 1920s saw a bubble in U.S. stocks, led by the exciting new technology of the motor car.

But the last few decades have seen an increase in bubble production. Gold formed a bubble that burst in 1980; Mexican and other Latin American debt suffered the same fate in 1982 and again in 1994; Japanese stocks peaked and collapsed in 1990, followed soon after by Scandinavian banking stocks; stocks of the Asian "Tiger" economies came back to earth in 1997; and the Internet bubble burst with the dot-com meltdown of 2000.[2]

Some said good news for the world economy had understandably created overenthusiasm. From 1950 to 2000, the world saw the renaissance of Germany and Japan, the peaceful end of the Cold War, and the rise of the emerging markets—all events that had seemed almost impossible in 1950—while young and growing populations poured money into stocks. Maybe the bubbles at the end of the century were nothing more than froth after an unrepeatable Golden Age.

But since then, the process has gone into overdrive. Bubbles in U.S. house prices and in U.S. mortgage-backed bonds, which started to burst in 2006, gave way to a bubble in Chinese stocks that burst in 2007. 2008 saw the bursting of bubbles in oil; industrial metals; foodstuffs; Latin American stocks; Russian stocks; Indian stocks; and even in currencies as varied as the Brazilian real, the pound sterling, and the Australian dollar. Then, 2009 brought one of the fastest rallies in history. News from the "real world" cannot possibly explain this.

Why have markets grown so much more prone to new bubbles? Overenthusiasm and herding behavior are part of human nature and it is fashionable to blame greed. But this makes little sense; it implies that people across the world have suddenly become greedier than they used to be. It is more accurate to say that in the last half century, fear has been stripped from investors' decisions. With greed no longer moderated by fear, investors are left with overconfidence.

This, I suggest, is thanks to what might be called the fearful rise of markets. The institutionalization of investment and the spread of markets to cover more of the global economy have inflated and synchronized bubbles. The rise of markets has brought the following trends in its wake.

Principal/Agent Splits

In the 1950s, investment was a game for amateurs, with less than 10 percent of the stocks on the New York Stock Exchange held by institutions; now institutions drive each day's trading. Lending was for professionals, with banks controlling virtually all decisions. Now that role has been taken by the capital markets. As economists put it, in both investing and lending, the "principals" have been split from the "agents." When people make decisions about someone else's money, they lose their fear and tend to take riskier decisions than they would with their own money.

Herding

The pressures on investors from the investment industry, and from their own clients, are new to this generation, and they magnify the already strong human propensity to crowd together in herds. Professional investors have strong incentives to crowd into investments that others have already made. When the weight of institutions' money goes to the same place at the same time, bubbles inflate.

Safety in Numbers

Not long ago, indexes were compiled weekly by teams of actuaries using slide rules. Stocks, without guaranteed dividends, were regarded as riskier than bonds. Now, mathematical models measure risk with precision, and show how to trade risk for return. Computers can perform the necessary calculations in milliseconds. The original theories were nuanced with many caveats, but their psychological impact on investors was cruder. They created the impression that markets could be understood and even controlled, and that led to overconfidence. They also promoted the idea that there was safety in investing in different assets, or diversification—an idea that encouraged taking risks and led investors into new markets they did not understand. This in turn tightened the links between markets.

Moral Hazard

As memories of the bank failures of the 1930s grew fainter, banks found ways around the limits imposed on them in that era, and governments eventually dismantled them altogether. Banks grew much bigger. Government bank rescues made money cheaper while fostering the impression among bankers that there would always be a rescue if they got into trouble. That created moral hazard—the belief that there would be no penalty for taking undue risks. Similarly, big bonuses for short-term performance, with no penalty or clawback for longer term losses, encouraged hedge fund managers and investment bankers to take big short-term risks and further boosted overconfidence.

The Rise of Markets and the Fall of Banks

Financial breakthroughs turned assets that were once available only to specialists into tradable assets that investors anywhere in the world could buy or sell at a second's notice with the click of a mouse. Emerging market stocks, currencies, credit, and commodities once operated in their separate walled gardens and followed their own rules. Now they are all interchangeable financial assets, and when their markets expanded with the influx of money, many risky assets shot upward simultaneously, forming synchronized bubbles. Meanwhile, banks, which had specialized in many of these areas, saw their roles usurped by markets. Rather than disappear, they sought new things to do—and were increasingly lured into speculative excesses.

These toxic ingredients combined to create the conditions for the now notorious mess in the U.S. subprime mortgage market, as financiers extended loans to people with no chance of repaying them, and then repackaged and dispersed those loans in such a way that nobody knew who was sitting on losses when the loans started to default. That led to a breakdown of trust in the U.S. financial system and—thanks to interconnected markets—global finance. Bad lending practices in Florida created a synchronized global crash.

This is not the place to dwell in detail on the subprime mess. Nobody now seriously questions that the absurdly complex financial engineering that undergirded it must not be repeated. It is much tougher, however, to deal with the conditions that made such a disaster possible. They are still in place and involve many worthwhile investment products we take for granted. Dealing with the problem at this level will involve very difficult choices.

As a start, I suggest we need rules to contain the most extreme behavior. Simply put, we must put fear back into the hearts of traders and investors, and force them to treat the money they are investing as if it were their own. The structure of the investment industry, which has evolved to reward and encourage herd-like behavior, must be rebuilt.

How markets rose to lead the world into such a synchronized mess is a fascinating but long story. As many of these themes overlap, I will cover them chronologically. But remember that bubbles are rooted in human psychology. It is inevitable that they will recur, but not inevitable that they need recur so swiftly or burst together, as they did in 2007 and 2008.

Part I

The Rise

Chapter 2

Investment Becomes an Industry

Brian: "You're all different!"
The crowd: "Yes, we ARE all different!"
Man in crowd: "I'm not."
The crowd: "Ssssh!"
Monty Python's Life of Brian

Investment has been institutionalized. Shares are now mostly bought and sold by institutions on behalf of someone else, not by individuals. Investors are judged by league tables, with a priority to maximize the amount of funds they manage rather than to make the biggest investment returns. With everyone trying to match the others, rather than stick out from the crowd, this drives them into "herding" behavior—and bubbles form where the herd goes.

What are investment managers paid to do? You might answer that they are paid to take their clients' money and make the best return they can, or to beat the market. But in fact, they are mostly paid to maximize the assets they have under management (rather than profits). Investment managers generate fees as a percentage of the amount of money they manage, so their greatest fear is that clients will pull money from the fund, not that the fund will perform badly. This has a huge impact on the way our money is invested; when motivated by this fear, managers try to do the same as everyone else instead of standing out from the crowd. Such behavior directly leads to bubbles.

It was not always that way. Not long ago, the U.S. stock market was almost entirely controlled by individuals and their families. According to the Federal Reserve, 90 percent of U.S. stocks were in the hands of households in 1952. As Figure 2.1 shows, by the end of 2008, they held less than 37 percent, while institutions held the rest. Stock market investing was once a game for wealthy individuals investing on their own account, but it is now an industry.

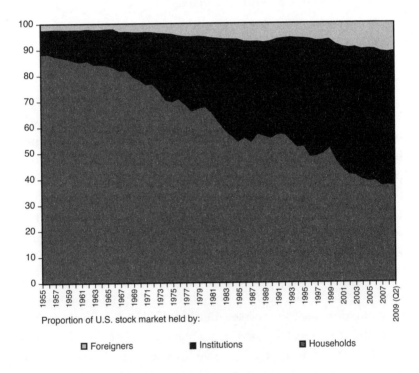

Proportion of U.S. stock market held by:

☐ Foreigners   ■ Institutions   ■ Households

Figure 2.1   *The institutionalization of the U.S. stock market*

It is easy to see how this happened. As the post-war Baby Boomers grew up, they put ever more money into generous public and corporate pension plans, which invested it in stocks. Companies set up to manage pension money offered their services directly to the public through mutual funds—big pools that take money from investors and invest it, with share prices that rise or fall in line with the value of fund's portfolio of stocks.

All of this makes sense. Investing in stocks is difficult and small savers need professionals to manage that money for them. But the investing "principals"—the savers trying to fund their retirement—have been separated from their "agents,"—the fund managers who run their money. Decisions by those agents, not the principals, now drive the market. The incentives they face push them to move together in and out of particular investments, and this helps inflate bubbles. If there is any single factor to explain the newfound propensity to form bubbles, it is this.

Like everyone else, investment managers respond to the way they are judged, and since the mid-1960s, they have been subjected to strict comparisons with their peers. Savers can find out easily on the Web how a fund ranks compared to its peers over the last few days or over many years. The trustees who control pension funds rely on a few global consulting firms for advice, and those consultants in turn are driven by league tables.

In theory, this should spur managers to do better than the rest, but in fact, it encourages herd behavior. Like wildebeest on the savannah, fund managers try to do the same as each other, not stand out from the herd. There is safety in numbers.

To illustrate how these twisted incentives work, let us look at the Fidelity Magellan Fund, which was launched in 1964 and is in many ways the model that the modern investment industry still follows. Fidelity aggressively advertised the great returns it made under Peter Lynch, its manager from 1977 to 1990. For example, in the 20 years from 1976 to 1996, Magellan gained 7,445 percent—far in excess of the S&P 500, the main U.S. stock market index, which gained only 1,311 percent.[1] After turning Lynch into a household name, Fidelity exported the formula, building in the UK on the back of the great track record of its star manager Anthony Bolton.

By the mid-1990s, Magellan was worth more than $50 billion, and Fidelity as a whole accounted for as much as 15 percent of each day's trading on the New York Stock Exchange. The problem for Jeffrey Vinik, Magellan's manager in 1995, was that Magellan was too big to make money the way it had done in the past. Sniffing out bargains in small stocks no longer helped. For example, if Magellan were to buy up all the stock of a company worth $100 million (an expensive operation in itself), and it doubled to $200 million, this would only grow the overall fund by 0.2 percent.

Magellan could not outperform its peers like that; it had to make bigger bets. And so in 1995, with the stock market rising, Vinik took about one-fifth of his portfolio out of stocks and put it into government bonds, in a bet that equities would soon fall. Instead, the stock market continued to boom, and the bonds killed Magellan's relative performance (although it kept growing thanks to the money it still held in stock). At its worst in 1996, its performance over the previous 12 months ranked it as number 590 out of 628 U.S. mutual funds aiming for growth from equities. Investors responded and for 14 consecutive months, as markets boomed, they pulled their money out.

Relative performance swamped everything else. Morningstar, a powerful U.S. fund-rating group, ranks all funds from one to five stars. In 1996, funds with five and four stars, making up less than one-third of all funds on offer, accounted for about 80 percent of all new money being invested. To lose such a high ranking by making a big bet like Vinik's and getting it wrong was career suicide.

Within months of making his bet, Vinik left Fidelity (and went on to have a brilliant second career running his own much smaller fund).[2] Robert Stansky, his successor (a former researcher for Peter Lynch), sold the bonds and bought big technology stocks instead. Technology was in vogue at the time, so it was hard to beat the market by much by investing in them. But that was not the point; the priority, if you do not want to lose your clients, is to avoid embarrassment. Holding the same stocks as everyone else means that if you lose money, all your competitors will do the same—which is much less damaging than losing out, Vinik-style, when everyone else is prospering. There is safety in numbers.

In 1997, Magellan closed its doors to new investors, admitting that the big flows of money were making it harder to perform. In 1999, it became the first mutual fund to hold more than $100 billion. That recovery, though, was rooted in doing what everyone else did, rather than in being different.

For Vinik, and other investment managers, size was the enemy of performance. And yet for managers, if not their clients, size is more important. Assets under management, not performance, determine how much they are paid. Thus it is hard to stop accepting new money from investors, as it means turning down revenues and profits. But letting funds grow too big encourages herding, which leads to bubbles. When investors poured money into Internet funds in the late 1990s, or into credit investments in 2006 and 2007, managers had to choose between putting more money into those investments, even if they thought them too expensive, or losing clients. Mostly, they chose to keep clients and kept buying—and as they bought, they pushed up prices, or inflated bubbles, even more.

Magellan also shows the dangers of standing out from the crowd. If Vinik's bet on a stock market fall had worked out, he might have attracted some more money. But often the response of pension funds' consultants when this happens is to take money out of recently successful funds so that they do not become too big a part of the portfolio. Meanwhile, of course, he ran the big risk of losing funds if he was wrong. The incentives on him were asymmetrical, with limited upside for a correct decision and severe downside for a mistake.

Other managers had the same problem. Jim Melcher, a New York fund manager, saw that Internet stocks were in a bubble in the 1990s, avoided them, and lost about 40 percent of his investors as a result. "We see it time and time again, especially in tough times," he said. "Major investors act like a flock of sheep with wolves circling them. They band closer and closer together. You want to be somewhere in the middle of that flock."[3]

Another problem was that by investing in bonds, rather than sticking to its customary stock-picking, Magellan had done something that investors had not expected. Savers wanted their managers to behave predictably. Moreover, brokers, sales representatives, and consultants, who controlled flows of money, want funds to stay within their assigned roles. By advising clients to spread their assets between different funds and shift them periodically, they can justify their existence.

As time went by, big mutual fund companies gained business by rigorously segmenting their funds, even if it encouraged managers to go against their better judgments and go with the herd. For example, a fund holding large companies was expected to maintain "style discipline" and not buy smaller companies, even if its manager thought smaller stocks would do better—a policy that again forced managers to crowd unwillingly into assets they thought were overpriced.

Magellan also illustrated that funds are judged and ranked based on short-term performance. Vinik's timing in 1995 was wildly off, as the stock market did not peak until 2000. Judging his move into bonds after 10 or 15 years, after two stock market crashes, it did not look so bad; but there is a human tendency to be swayed by recent performance and to expect it to continue. Clients tend to put their money into funds that have done well recently, often buying at the top and selling at the bottom.

Attempts to time turning points in the markets can be a professional kiss of death. Just look at the roll call of managers who predicted the collapse of Internet stocks, probably the biggest stock market mania of all time. Paul Woolley, who managed the UK operations for the large U.S. fund manager GMO, was rewarded by sweeping redemptions. He is now a professor at the London School of Economics, where he used his money to endow the Centre for Capital Market Dysfunctionality. The late Tony Dye, once head of the London fund manager UBS Phillips & Drew, earned himself the nickname of "Dr. Doom" and lost his job in February 2000, weeks before the bubble burst.[4] They were proved right by history, but they would have been better off if they had gone with the herd and stayed in stocks. The same is true of the (very few) fund managers who stayed away from the credit bubble before the implosion of 2007 and 2008.

While funds were restricted to stocks, herding manifested itself in manias for particular kinds of stocks—conglomerates in the 1960s, technology stocks in the 1990s, and banking stocks in the middle of the 2000s. As funds widened to include different assets, including commodities and foreign exchange, and cover most of the world, the herd started to move across the globe, leaving ever larger and more synchronized bubbles behind them.

Indexes guided them on their path.

In Summary

- Institutionalized investment pushes investors to move in herds: Paying fund managers a percentage of the assets they manage and judging them against peers encourages them all to do the same thing.
- Solutions might include paying a flat rate and finding new benchmarks based on skill.

Chapter 3

Indexes and Efficient Markets

"The investment management business is built upon a simple and basic belief: professional managers can beat the market. That premise appears to be false."

Charles D. Ellis, Financial Analysts Journal, July 1975

Index funds are a great idea for most investors, but the more they grow, the more inefficient they make the market, and the more they encourage investors to move in lockstep. They are based on academic theories on efficient markets which breed a psychology of overconfidence, that inflates bubbles.

Index funds—normal mutual funds that merely match the returns of an index, rather than trying to beat it—are dull staple products that make investing much cheaper for small savers. But they have only been around since 1975 and have their roots in a radical academic theory that holds that it is impossible to beat the market.

The irony is that as they grow more successful, they make the market less efficient. This should make it easier for active managers to beat the index. And yet the response of active managers has instead been to herd ever closer to the index.

Index funds also enable the kind of "top-down" investing, based on big international trends, that has inflated global super-bubbles. While virtually every investor should hold some index funds, the painful paradox is that they have helped make markets much more prone to bubbles.

Let us look at how index funds developed. Jack Bogle is the father of the index fund, an idea that came to him as a driven young Princeton academic who wrote a thesis questioning whether fund managers could beat the market. Unperturbed by the lack of demand from investors, he launched the first S&P 500 index fund in 1975, primarily on the proposition that index funds should be cheap.[1] He modeled the ethos of his company, Vanguard, on a ship at sea (it has "crew members," not employees) and adopted a structure aimed at minimizing principal-agent conflicts; the management company itself belongs to the mutual funds it manages.

Fund managers typically spend heavily on research to piece together portfolios with maybe a hundred stocks in them. If the efficient markets hypothesis, which was developed in U.S. universities in the 1950s and 1960s, is correct, this money is wasted. Stock prices always incorporate all known information, so their movements are random and cannot be predicted from one day to the next. They follow a "random walk."[2] Therefore, there is no point in paying for expensive research.

Computers offered an alternative. The S&P 500 index includes 500 stocks. Taking in money and paying out redemptions each day and buying or selling the right amount of stocks to track the index was impossible for fund managers armed with slide rules, but is easily done with computers, at much lower costs than active funds incur when they try to beat the market. Running index funds has grown cheaper as computers get more powerful and the funds grow bigger. For index funds, size is not the enemy of performance, as they enjoy economies of scale.

Bogle proved to be right about indexing. From 1978 to 1998, the S&P outperformed 79 percent of all mutual funds that survived that long—and this excludes those wound up due to poor performance. In the 30 years to December 2008, the S&P returned 11 percent per year, against 9.3 percent for active equity mutual funds.[3]

Investors saw this and bought in. Vanguard's S&P 500 index fund grew to be worth more than $100 billion, and overtook Magellan as the world's biggest fund in 2000, while Vanguard itself overtook Fidelity to become the biggest mutual fund manager in the United States.

Bogle changed investing. To see how, we must look at the theories that, in conjunction with the "random walk," appeared to unlock the central mysteries of investing.[4]

Central notions are that risk can be quantified, and that risk and return can be traded off precisely to come up with an asset allocation that balances them. Risk is defined by how volatile a security's price is; stocks that are prone to wide leaps and dives are riskier than stable stocks, even if in the long run their return is better.

To deal with risk, the theory holds that we should look at how much one security's returns are correlated with another's. If you have two very volatile stocks with strong returns, holding two will be less risky than holding one, provided that they are not correlated with each other, because the odds are that when one falls the other one will be alright. The art of risk management then becomes to add more securities until it is no longer possible to boost your return without also boosting your risk. Provided that the correlations are low, you can add a risky security to your portfolio, and make it less risky. These insights can all be quantified with elegant mathematics, and they have led investors for a generation on a hunt for assets with a low correlation to the assets they already hold. This drove them, as we will see, to create a synchronized bubble; once investors held on to assets on the assumption that they were uncorrelated, they tended to become correlated.

Another key concept is that market returns will follow the bell curve distribution that often occurs in natural sciences. Human height, for example, follows a bell curve. Applied to the market, it implies that a graph of daily stock market returns should follow a smooth curve (see Figure 3.1). Most days' returns will be close to the average or have a small rise. A few days there will be outliers of very bad or very good returns. These are known in the jargon as the "tails." But the key is that everything follows the smooth outlines of a bell, with steadily tapering thin tails. The more extreme the event, whether positive or negative, the less likely it is to occur. Armed with these theories and some data, investors can approach each day with a precise figure for the maximum amount of money they are likely to lose that day.

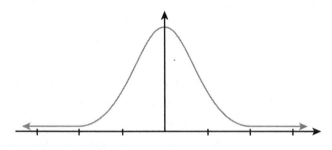

Figure 3.1   *The bell curve—safety in numbers*

How seriously did real practitioners take the academic ideas? The "random walk," as Bogle spotted, implies that active management is pointless. Any real-life investors who continued to manage funds actively must therefore have assumed that these theories were at best an approximation of reality. Real life, with its booms and busts, shows that the "random walk" is not a perfect model, although it often holds good during long periods of stability. But even though investors knew that markets were not perfectly efficient, they used models based on that assumption to pick stocks and to manage risk.

More importantly, regulators forced them to take the academics seriously In 1974, Congress passed ERISA, the Employee Retirement Income Savings Act, which revolutionized the business of managing pension funds first in the United States and then elsewhere. The act required investment managers to be "prudent," and it defined that word to mean that they should manage money in line with modern portfolio theory. This exacerbated still further their tendency to move in herds.

Most importantly, the theories became central to the curriculum of all business schools and had a psychological effect. By putting a precise number on risk, they diminished MBA students' fear of the unknown. This turned to overconfidence, even when they reached trading desks and found the theories did not work as neatly in practice as they had done at business school. Bogle himself diagnosed this, saying he did not believe that "this focus on simplistic mathematical precision is a healthy state of being for managers, nor for their clients, nor for the market itself."[5]

All of this matters because the structure rests on unsafe foundations. Risk, it turns out, cannot be measured with mathematical precision. Security price movements are not random, and extreme moves are far more common than the bell curve suggests. Benoit Mandelbrot, a Polish *émigré* mathematician best known as the inventor of fractal geometry, proved this as early as 1962. Studying financial markets as a hobby, he graphed daily stock and commodity price movements and looked for patterns. They were clearly not random, as there were too many extreme events, and he published a paper on cotton prices making this clear. "Bubbles and crashes are inherent to markets," Mandelbrot argued. They were "the inevitable consequence of the human need to find patterns in the patternless."[6]

Moreover, extreme events account for the bulk of all performance. From 1916 to 2003, on the assumption that markets followed a bell curve, there should have been 58 days when the Dow Jones Industrial Average, the oldest U.S. stock index, moved more than

3.4 percent. There were in fact 1,001. Index swings of 7 percent should come along once every 300 years, but made an appearance 48 times in the twentieth century alone.

But when Mandelbrot published his critique in 1962, academic economists denigrated it. They did this, arguably, because the bell curve was convenient for them. By assuming basic randomness, markets and risk management could be brought within the realm of conventional mathematics, opening all kinds of avenues to further research. If Mandelbrot was right, markets could only be modeled with the mind-bendingly complex mathematics needed to measure wind turbulence or chaos, which is even now still in its infancy. And so academics ignored Mandelbrot and cheerfully carried on building models on the assumption that price moves were random.[7]

"It does not work as advertised," Mandelbrot commented sourly, but "it gives a comforting impression of precision and competence." But anywhere the bell curve assumption entered "an error came out.... It means stock portfolios are being put together incorrectly; far from managing risk, they may be magnifying it."[8]

Markets became less efficient when driven by ideas based on efficiency. Even index funds are a force for inefficiency, as they make no attempt to spot which stocks are over- or under-valued, and instead accept the market's judgment. When bubbles start, index funds automatically buy more overpriced stocks, and sell stocks that are underpriced. If internet stocks are rising and displacing industries that generate real profits, then index funds must dumbly buy them and make the mispricing all the worse. If managers at a company misbehave, index funds do nothing to stop them, even though the capitalist system relies on shareholders, the companies' owners, to enforce good behavior.

"Fundamental indexing," in which funds track indexes based on the fundamentals of a stock—such as its earnings or dividends rather than on its market value—maintains the low costs of indexing, but does not chase the market into overvalued stocks. This helps avoid herding tendency and contributes to strong performance in the longer term. So, this development could play a major role in dealing with the problem, but for now fundamental index funds are only a very small part of the market.

Markets need active managers to conduct research and make sure prices stay realistic. This creates the paradox that as individual investors buy more index funds, they introduce inefficiencies, creating opportunities for active managers. But active managers tend not to take this opportunity. Instead, index funds increase the pressure to seek safety in numbers. By hugging to the stocks in the index, a fund ensures that it will not lose too badly relative to the market, even if their clients would be far better off in a cheaper pure index fund, where they pay no research costs.

The most famous alleged "closet indexer" was Magellan itself. Robert Stansky's changes to the fund made it look ever more like the index. Antti Petajisto, a finance professor at Yale, came up with a concept to measure this, which he calls the "active share." This measures the fraction of a fund's holdings that differ from the S&P 500—for example, if its holdings are identical except that it has no Microsoft, which is 4 percent of the S&P, and instead holds 4 percent in stocks outside the index, it has an "active share" of 4 percent. A pure index fund has an active share of zero. An equity fund that invests only in obscure stocks excluded from the index has an active share of 100 percent.

Under Peter Lynch in the 1970s, Mr. Petajisto showed, Magellan had an active share of more than 90 percent. When the fund was smaller it had truly been able to buy bargains far from the mainstream. After Jeff Vinik's bet on bonds, the active share was 77 percent—still plainly a very different beast from the index. Under Stansky, the active share fell to 33 percent.[9] Stansky denied suggestions that he was a "closet indexer," saying that he was not afraid to make any bet. And over his first five years, he slightly outperformed the S&P. But his own account of his success showed the gravitational pull that the index exerts on fund managers. "How do you beat the S&P?" he asked an interviewer rhetorically. "You beat it by over-weighting some groups, underweighting others, and by owning stocks that aren't in the S&P."[10]

Psychologists identify "framing" as a persistent problem leading to bad decisions. Once we frame an issue in a particular way, it is hard to approach it differently, and indexes now frame the perceptions of many "active" investors. Fund managers describe themselves as "over-weight" or "underweight" a stock or sector, by comparing its weight within their fund to its weight within the index. Compilers of the most widely tracked indexes, such as Dow Jones, S&P, MSCI Barra, and FTSE, have grown hugely powerful. Stockbrokers devote reams of research to predicting changes in indexes; stocks jump when they are included in a major index and plummet when they are excluded.

Research by Mr. Petajisto and others shows that indexes have come to dominate all fund management. Pure index funds grew from 1 to about 15 percent of mutual fund assets during the 1990s, but the fraction of "closet indexers" (with an active share of between 20 and 60 percent) rose to about 30 percent of all assets in 2003, compared to almost zero in the 1980s. This has indeed created opportunities for those who are truly active. Mr. Petajisto's research shows funds with the highest active share beating their index by more than one percent-age point a year, even after expenses.[11] But for fund managers, the urge to herd was too strong, and most spurned the opportunity.

Bogle himself scorned "investment relativism," and described closet indexing as the most "ineffective" response possible to indexing. "Today's chance of victory, as small as it demonstrably is for active managers, will become tomorrow's certainty of defeat if managers offer tacit index funds with high fees," he said. It also helped make bubbles more certain—and the rise of markets soon ensured that this approach spread from stock investment to the price of money itself. Once set by banks, for many of us the price of a loan is now set by markets.

In Summary

- Index investing is a good idea for most savers, but it makes markets more inefficient and prone to bubbles, as index funds must buy into stocks that are overvalued and avoid stocks that are out of fashion.
- Its popularity also encouraged "closet indexing" by active managers.
- Theories of market efficiency, despite fundamental flaws, stoked overconfidence.
- They led many investors to look for assets that had low historic correlations to stocks they already held—spreading the reach of correlated markets.
- For savers, the solution is a rigid division; either buy an index fund or buy a fund that is truly active.
- And for professional investors the need is for a new theory of investment.

Chapter 4

Money Markets Supplant Banks

> *"We are pleased to report that you, and the markets in general, have embraced the very concept and foundation on which The Reserve was founded, an unwavering discipline focused on protecting your principal, providing daily liquidity and transparency, and all the while boring you into a sound sleep."*
>
> Bruce Bent, chairman of the Reserve Fund in July 2008, weeks before his fund took a loss on bonds issued by Lehman Brothers[1]

Capital markets took over the core functions of banks, with money market funds even offering checkbooks. This left decisions about lending to the market, with its big swings of sentiment, rather than to banks' lending officers, and forced banks to find new lines of business. This stoked speculation as banks poured money into areas that were new to them.

Banking underwent the same change as investment, as the market split the principals from their agents. In 1975, Merrill Lynch launched its Ready Assets money market fund, one of the most boring financial instruments ever invented. A money market fund is like any other mutual fund: it invests solely in the money markets—certificates of deposit, bank deposits, or very short-term bonds. These instruments carry negligible risk, but their high minimum investments put them beyond the reach of most investors. Funds got around this by holding a big portfolio of such deposits, and then offering shares, with a much smaller minimum investment, to small investors. Even after the fees the fund charged, small investors could earn a higher interest rate.

The first such fund, The Reserve Fund, was launched in 1969. Merrill Lynch now added a crucial marketing twist: a checkbook. Henceforward, its clients could treat money market funds exactly like bank accounts, pulling out money instantly. It was a stunning success. In its first year, savers poured in as interest rates rose, taking Merrill's fund from 1.6 million to 8.1 million shares, or from $8 billion to $40 billion in assets.[2] By 1982, as inflation and interest rates finally came under control, the burgeoning money market fund industry controlled $207 billion in deposits.

Without a branch network to keep up, without the regulated interest rates imposed on banks, and with no premiums to pay for deposit insurance, money market funds had drastically lower costs than banks. To maintain the sense among clients that this was really a bank account by another name, they maintained a constant share price of $1.00, with all gains accruing as interest.

But despite appearances, they were not bank accounts. Instead, they removed power from banks and gave it to markets. By not having to pay for deposit insurance, one of their critical advantages, money market funds were an end run around one of the critical Depression-era reforms to rebuild confidence in the banks. Without insurance, there was a (very small) danger that the investments they held might default or fall in value to bring the fund's share price below $1.00. "Breaking the buck" would show the funds to be riskier than bank accounts.

Paul Volcker, legendary head of the Federal Reserve, the U.S. central bank, was a cynic. In 2009, he made clear that he thought they should be subject to the same restrictions as banks: "They didn't exist before, and they exist as a pure regulatory arbitrage. They promise to return at par. You can write checks against it. That's what demand deposits in banks do, and money market funds can do it without the inconvenience of reserve requirements and all the other regulatory requirements."[3]

Regulators did codify some new requirements. In 1983, the Securities and Exchange Commission set rules on the credit quality of the bonds the funds could hold, along with their maturity and their diversification, and ensured that the funds had to be able to sell their investments quickly if necessary. Provided the funds kept to these guidelines, they could keep the value of each share pegged at $1.00. In other words, they could realistically aim never to lose money. Even though they were not insured, the rules bolstered the impression that they were, leading to a further explosion in the uses to which the funds were put. Money markets funds became a parking area for the global investment community.

Money moved in and out of them at staggering speed. In the 25 years after the SEC adopted its rule, the period that saw the growth of the super-bubble, $325 trillion flowed in and out of money market funds.[4] (The gross domestic product of the entire planet in 2009 was about $70 trillion.) Meanwhile, the assets held in the funds rose almost without interruption and grew far faster than the economy. By 1997, they topped $1 trillion for the first time. By 2008, they held $3.8 trillion. During this time, banks themselves developed arcane structures using the same principles as money market funds— borrowing in the short-term and putting the proceeds into longer-term bonds—until they had created what has come to be known as the "shadow banking system," accessible only to the world's biggest bankers.

These new financial beasts needed to be fed. States and cities could now borrow money much more easily, by issuing bonds and selling them to money market funds. The funds were also buyers of commercial paper: very short-term loans to big companies, which would previously have been made by banks. Generally the terms of these loans were so short that default was not an issue—a big company may default in the next 20 years, but almost certainly not in the next month. Because the funds had much lower overheads than banks, they would let the companies borrow at a lower interest rate.

So far, so good. Through alert financial engineering, the costs of borrowing for almost everyone in the economy had been reduced and savers could get a higher rate of return on money that would have otherwise been parked doing nothing. Lenders and borrowers alike could avoid paying for the big overheads incurred by heavily regulated banks.

But there were issues. The credit of an American state, or of a very large company, is very strong, but it is not quite as strong as that of the U.S. government or of a bank deposit. That is why they pay slightly higher interest. While low-risk, these funds were not riskless. That implied that every so often, a default might force a fund to take a loss and mark its share price down below $1.00. Further, the funds were competing with each other. A higher rate of return would generate more business while also increasing risk. And they had improved on the banks in large part by avoiding the regulations designed to ensure that banks did not crash. Did that mean they could tolerate "breaking the buck"?

It soon turned out that the answer was "no." Instead of "more return for a little more risk," their proposition was to be "more return for no more risk." Several times during the 1990s, money market funds found themselves holding securities that fell in value, and on each occasion they were bailed out by their management companies. As money market funds tended to be controlled by large fund management companies with many other sources of revenue, and their losses tended to be very small, this could be done easily. Ultimately the owners of the management company, and not the investors in the funds, would take a small hit. With each successive incident, the impression took hold that the funds could not in any situation lose money.

One exception came in 1994, after the bankruptcy of Orange County in southern California, when The Community Bankers U.S. Government Money-Market Fund took a loss and opted to close itself down, paying shareholders 94 cents for each dollar they had put in. But this fund did not have a large management company to give it an implicit guarantee, and held only $82 million, a tiny amount for a money fund. The incident passed without seriously denting investors' confidence.

By making money cheaper without making it seem riskier, or by fostering the impression that there would always be a bail-out if risks went wrong, these developments encouraged the funds' managers and their investors to take greater risks—a concept known to economists as "moral hazard" that has now grown painfully familiar. These practices also boosted the supply of money available to pour into riskier assets—and thereby stoked speculation. By persuading investors to keep money that would otherwise be kept on deposit in insured vehicles, they also raised the risk of a bank run, or sudden loss of confidence in banks.

At a collective level, there was another problem. In many ways, the funds—and the many structures like them in the shadow banking system—were using the safety that comes in the short-term as a means to manage risk. Healthy companies simply do not default in a matter of days or weeks. This increased the temptation for investment banks seeking funding to borrow over very short periods. This cut the interest they paid and made it easier for the investment banks to make money; but it also meant that if the funds stopped lending to them (by refusing to buy their commercial paper), they could run out of money very quickly. This made the financial system less stable, as the world discovered when the synchronized bubble finally burst in 2007 and 2008.

Another crucial side effect of the rise of money markets was to strip banks of their main business. If banks were not the best in the business of offering checking accounts to customers at competitive interest rates, or at lending to big companies over short periods, what was their point?

These businesses had once belonged to the commercial banks. Lending officers would decide whether to make short-term loans. Now the same transaction came in the form of the company selling commercial paper to money market funds. The market set the price. With all its capacity for herding and overreaction, the market had taken over the job once done by individuals working in banks.

Bank executives could respond to money market funds either by shrinking their banks to acknowledge their newly diminished role, or by scrambling to find something else to do. Human nature dictated that few wanted to do the first. Therefore, banks scrambled to find new sources of profit, such as lending to emerging markets, real estate developers, corporate raiders, or subprime mortgage lenders—a roll call of the speculative excesses of the last 30 years. Many of these booms and busts were driven by banks looking for something new to do and finding themselves in rocky and unfamiliar terrain.

And so, just like index funds, money market funds embody a paradox. The case for individual investors to invest in them is overwhelming. Indeed, there is little reason not to; they are like bank accounts, which everyone needs, and they pay more money for barely any more risk. But collectively, they bolstered overconfidence and provided an incentive for everyone to fund themselves on a dangerously short-term basis. Their role was all the more important because the value of money is no longer linked to gold.

In Summary

- Money market funds took key business away from banks and gave it to markets. They provide cheaper financing for companies and higher rates for savers.
- But money market funds made bank runs more likely by avoiding deposit insurance and encouraging banks to rely on shorter-term financing. Management companies created moral hazard by intervening to stop them from "breaking the buck."
- Regulating and insuring funds like banks might deal with these problems.

Chapter 5

From Gold Standard to Oil Standard

> *"Having behind us the commercial interests and the laboring interests and all the toiling masses, we shall answer their demands for a gold standard by saying to them, you shall not press down upon the brow of labor this crown of thorns. You shall not crucify mankind upon a cross of gold."*
>
> William Jennings Bryan, July 9, 1896, National Democratic Convention

Leaving the gold standard in 1971 was a necessary condition for the booms and busts that followed. With gold as an anchor, exchange rates barely move. Without the gold standard, currencies depend on the credibility of central banks. And if central banks lose their credibility, the world's anchor is the price of oil, not gold.

Gold is scarce. If all the gold that has ever been produced and sold were melted down, it would fit into a cube with sides 20 meters long. This valuable object would fit into the hold of a modern tanker. But gold is an unusually dense metal, so the tanker would sink.

This scarcity has for centuries made gold a coveted asset. But it has never been so coveted as it was in 1980, when a frenzy to buy gold coins pushed the price up to $850 per ounce, 24 times higher than the price of $35 per ounce, at which it had been fixed for decades until 1971. This was the world's first investment bubble of the post-war era, and it was inflated by opportunistic political fixes that fundamentally shifted the world's financial dynamics. It made it possible for diverse markets to overheat at once, forming a synchronized bubble.

Gold once anchored the world's financial system. Once unmoored, the capitalist world suffered a decade of "stagflation" (inflation combined with stagnation) before it regained kilter. The key elements of the new system that has evolved are that the value of money rests on the credibility of central banks; that exchange rates, which set the terms of international trade, are set by markets, not governments; and that the price of oil has replaced the price of gold as the system's anchor.

Until 1971, the capitalist world followed rules set at the summit the victorious allied powers held in the New Hampshire resort of Bretton Woods in 1944. They returned to the system that had been in place for much of history, where paper banknotes in circulation carried the guarantee that they could be exchanged for a certain amount of gold. As gold is scarce, that put strict limits on the amount of money that governments could print. The aftermath of the First World War, when Germany had lapsed into hyperinflation as it printed money to pay its war debts, suggested to the leaders that this was necessary.

Under the Bretton Woods system, the gold price was fixed in dollars at $35 per ounce, and other currencies' exchange rates were fixed to the dollar. Hence gold anchored all currencies, which remained broadly fixed against each other. The money supply was limited so it was hard for inflation to rise. During the Bretton Woods era, the capitalist world largely avoided banking crises, and investment bubbles. Economic growth was steady, although punctuated by recessions. But the system was a straitjacket for governments with expensive ambitions, and put the onus on the United States to be the banker for the entire capitalist world. This became harder and harder.

By 1971, the gold standard was having much the same effect on the U.S. economy as a cube of gold might have on a supertanker.

Foreign governments, ever keener to convert their dollars into gold, had outstanding claims of $36 billion against only $18 billion in gold reserves that the United States had put aside for the purpose.[1] Meanwhile, the costs of the Vietnam War and the expansive social programs of the 1960s weighed on the budget. And Richard Nixon, the incumbent president, wanted to be re-elected the following year.

The United States had already resorted to numerous fixes to balance the books, but the numbers did not add up. After a momentous summer weekend at the presidential retreat in Camp David, Nixon announced with little fanfare that foreigners could no longer exchange their paper dollars for gold. Nixon portrayed the move as a "triumph and a fresh start."[2]

By doing this, he stood in a populist American tradition of opposition to the gold standard that stretched back at least as far as the presidential candidate William Jennings Bryan, who in 1896 proclaimed that the United States was "crucified on a cross of gold" and demanded to adulterate the currency and boost the money supply by mixing in silver.

In the short-term, Nixon's closing of the gold window was an economic master-stroke of the kind Bryan probably envisaged, as it allowed for a pump-priming expansion. Nixon imposed price controls so the Federal Reserve did not have to worry about inflation. There was nothing to stop it printing more money. The total money supply rose by about 10 percent in 1971 (the greatest increase on record), the economy grew by an impressive 5 percent the following year, and Nixon won re-election.

This quick fix highlights many of the gold standard's problems. Demand for gold is itself irrational—its value is almost entirely in the eye of the beholder. Any new discovery can cause a dramatic increase in its supply. And yet under a gold standard, these factors critically affect the supply of money in the economy. As more and more countries came into the capitalist fold in the 1990s, the world could not possibly have remained tied to gold. The concept was hopelessly outdated.

But the gold standard needed a replacement. Without a link to gold, a currency is merely a creation of governmental fiat. Its strength resides in the reputation of its central bankers. It is not obvious that this is much better, and it creates opportunities to bet against central banks that investors have come to exploit ruthlessly. The investment writer James Grant, a well-known supporter of the gold standard, is scathing: "To strike off a half-ton of a new currency on a printing press takes no great skill. The history of inflation attests to it. Digging up gold out of the earth is a much harder proposition, which is exactly what commended the gold standard to our monetary forebears."[3]

Far from happening in a vacuum, Nixon's neat opportunism changed the rules of world trade. The effect on the dollar was instant. Within months the gold price had moved from $35 per ounce to $44 per ounce. Trading partners who had been holding on to piles of dollars found that they bought 25 percent less gold. This ended the Bretton Woods era. Currencies floated, exchange rates diverged, and the world soon experienced the first swing of the balancing system that has remained in place ever since. It is now run by the oil market.

As far as the oil exporters on whom the United States depended were concerned, Nixon had just slashed the amount of gold that they received for their oil. From 1971 to late 1973, the price in gold of a barrel dropped by two-thirds. This in part drove the OPEC cartel of mostly Middle-Eastern oil producers to triple oil prices in October 1973, a move that triggered the great 1970s stagflation. And as U.S. inflation increased, so the value of the dollar weakened, spurring a second OPEC oil price hike at the end of the decade.

The price of oil in terms of gold suggests that the oil producers had little choice but to raise prices (see Figure 5.1).

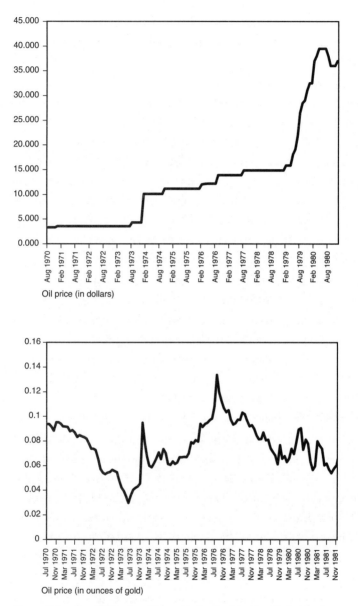

Oil price (in dollars)

Oil price (in ounces of gold)

Figure 5.1   *The 1970s: from the gold standard to the oil standard*

As the charts show, the price of oil in dollars may have gone through the roof in the 1970s, but when priced in gold, it was stable— the two great price hikes merely attempted to adjust for the weakened buying power of the dollar. In November 1979, an ounce of gold bought 12 barrels of oil, compared to about 11 barrels in 1971 under the gold standard. Having abandoned the gold standard, the United States found itself instead tied to a new "oil standard."

OPEC's actions in turn inflated the bubble in gold. As inflation took hold, investors desperately bought up gold coins, believing this was the only way to hold on to value—perhaps validating the James Grant view that the gold price is "the reciprocal of the world's faith in the stewards of paper money." With fear rampant, investors' loss of confidence in central bankers was extreme. It also gave rise to a wave of speculation, as investors started to pay prices for gold that showed they were betting on the behavior of others, rather than calculating a sensible price for the metal. That is how an ounce of gold went from $35 to $850 in only nine years.

Getting out of the dynamic, like getting into it, rested on a minor act of political expediency. In the summer of 1979, President Jimmy Carter was in trouble, rocked by the deep economic malaise. Reshuffling his cabinet in a bid to revive his fortunes, he had difficulty finding a new treasury secretary, and eventually gave the job to the incumbent head of the Federal Reserve. That left a hole at the Fed, which terrified the markets. Carter's advisers hurried to find a replacement, and after a weekend of consulting Wall Streeters, decided that Paul Volcker, an economist and lifelong civil servant who then ran the New York Fed, was the best bet to steady the markets. A hasty appointment installed the man who would prove to embody a new gold standard.

Volcker acted drastically to restore confidence in the dollar, raising interest rates repeatedly, squeezing out the credit from the system and forcing the United States into another recession. Markets nosedived.

By the summer of 1982, Volcker's harsh medicine had engineered such a bear market in stocks that they were worth no more, after inflation, than they had been in 1954. Unemployment hit 10.8 percent.[4]

By going to such extremes, Volcker had earned credibility. His remedy was a blunt instrument, like the gold standard itself, but markets could believe in the value of a paper dollar backed by a Fed that behaved this way. With no fear of inflation, investors did not demand high interest rates on long-term bonds, so rates fell. And so the longest bull market for stocks in history got under way.

The international dynamics that followed Nixon's devaluation of the dollar with an oil spike and a recession remain in place. Traders now know that a weaker dollar, or higher inflation, will mean higher oil prices. If they fear higher U.S. inflation, therefore, they will buy oil. Unlike gold, oil is plentiful. Tankers full of it ply their trade around the world. But unlike gold, it is central to the workings of an industrial economy, and big swings in its price wreak havoc. The new *de facto* "oil standard" was destabilizing in the 1970s, and it was again in 2008 and 2009. This relationship led to the synchronized markets of the twenty-first century.

The growing importance of oil also had another consequence: It drove more money toward lesser developed countries that had previously been excluded from the capitalist system. In the 1980s they became ever more tightly linked.

In Summary

- The economically vital markets for oil and foreign exchange are tightly linked. Under the gold standard, they were external to the market, set by governments; now markets determine them.

- A gold standard is probably unworkable in the twenty-first century, but it thwarted excessive devaluations and inflation and would have thwarted the growth of synchronized bubbles.

- Its place has been taken by oil; devaluation and inflation now lead to oil prices so high that they dampen world growth.
- Investors now treat oil as a great hedge against devaluation and inflation.

Chapter 6

Emerging Markets

> *"The other boys at Yale came from wealthy families, and none of them were investing outside the United States, and I thought, 'That is very egotistical. Why be so shortsighted or nearsighted as to focus only on America? Shouldn't you be more open-minded?'"*
>
> Emerging markets pioneer Sir John Templeton

The launch of investment funds to buy shares in emerging stock markets created a new asset class and allowed investors easily to pull money in and out of the developing world for the first time. Before this, emerging markets were totally uncorrelated with developed markets; by 2009, they moved in lockstep.

Until 1982, financing for the world's Lesser Developed Countries (LDCs) was driven by commodity prices and western banks. As rising oil prices created greater wealth and western banks looked for new sources of business, banks came to make variable-rate loans directly to emerging countries' governments—not their companies. José López Portillo, then president of Mexico, told his people they should "learn how to administer abundance" as he expanded oil production, while the banks financing this took refuge in the belief that countries do not go bust.

But in 1982 the LDCs model collapsed, after Mexico was forced to devalue its currency and then renegotiate its debt with lenders—a pattern that then repeated across Latin America. Within a year, there came a radical new way to invest outside the developed world. In place of lending to the LDCs, there arose the Emerging Markets, as the fund management industry started to offer pooled investments in exotic stock exchanges. This had huge consequences for what had been known as the Third World. It also changed investors' behavior and contributed to the synchronized expansion and contraction of markets around the world. In the 1980s, emerging markets and the developed world had nothing to do with each other and were totally uncorrelated; by 2009, the correlation between them was almost perfect.

What drove this shift? Mexico, then the biggest and most advanced of the emerging markets, suffered from misguided ambitions, which bankers in the United States were only too happy to finance. They desperately needed new source of business to replace the revenues they were losing to the commercial paper market at home. While Paul Volcker was making money expensive in the United States, it was much easier to look for bargains elsewhere.

The banks also had a lot of money to invest. The oil price spike had left the big oil-producing nations of OPEC with surplus funds, generally labeled petro-dollars, which they deposited in the banks of the United States and Western Europe. Faced with swollen coffers, banks behaved irresponsibly—a phenomenon that recurred during the next great oil spike in 2007 and 2008.

LDCs gave the petro-dollars a natural home. The Third World had been growing steadily since the 1960s, and its need for financing ratcheted up after the 1973 oil spike pushed up their costs. López Portillo was not the only Latin American leader eager to accept the banks' terms. And so money poured from U.S. banks into Latin America, and particularly Mexico. At the end of 1970, Latin America owed a total of $29 billion. By the end of 1978, on the eve of the second oil spike, it owed $159 billion. By the 1982 crisis, the region's indebtedness doubled again, to $327 billion.[1] Banks clubbed together to make the loans, which had a variable interest rate, and were denominated in dollars, meaning repayments could rise sharply if a country's currency devalued. Rather than investing in companies, the game was to lend to national governments on the basis that, in the words of Walter Wriston, who led Citicorp at the time, "The country does not go bankrupt. Any country, no matter how badly off, will 'own' more than it 'owes.'"[2]

But in some circumstances, countries do go bust. The circumstances that led Mexico and the U.S. banks into each other's arms in the first place also bore the seeds of eventual disaster. The money ignited an unsustainable boom in Mexico, where inflation took hold. Meanwhile higher rates and lower inflation in the United States under Volcker pushed up the value of the dollar, and with it the cost for Mexicans of servicing their debt. López Portillo vowed to defend the peso "like a dog," but in the summer of 1982, just as the U.S. stock market started to rise, he had no choice but to devalue. That meant disaster for Mexico and its creditors, which deepened when the president nationalized all of Mexico's banks.[3]

Where Mexico led, others followed. By October 1983, 27 countries were rescheduling their debt, and the Latin American region entered what is now known as the "lost decade." Meanwhile, a Mexican currency crisis soon spurred a U.S. banking crisis. Mexico, Brazil, Venezuela, and Argentina owed $37 billion between them to the eight largest banks in the United States. This was almost 50 percent more than those banks held in capital and reserves at the time. These crises took nearly a decade to resolve as countries renegotiated loans, while U.S. regulators allowed banks to limp along on life support rather than forcing them to recognize all their losses. This lenient treatment arguably encouraged greater risk-taking for the future.

The LDCs crisis set a pattern that has now been repeated several times. U.S. banks showed a knack for making massive loans that they knew might not be repaid. Problems for the poor, in this case Latin Americans, soon translated themselves into problems for the wealthy (big U.S. banks). High commodity prices blurred judgments and drove excessive flows of money into small markets, thus destabilizing them. And the motors that drove the crisis, far from Mexico, were the international price of oil and the state of the credit market in the United States. All these conditions recurred in the crisis of 2008.

But in 1982, the World Bank had a more immediate problem: How could the world's poorer nations finance their rapid growth? Lending to them was dangerous, and the countries themselves badly needed to reduce their reliance on debt. Antoine van Agtmael, a young Belgian official at the World Bank, thought that investing directly in growing companies would be more appealing. If things went well, there was far more "upside," or potential profit to be made. And if things did not go well, it would be far easier for companies to skip a dividend payment than to default on a loan.

The job of vetting and valuing companies in countries like Brazil or South Korea, however, was prohibitively expensive for most investors. Often such companies did not even have recognizable balance sheets or accounting standards. Political, cultural, and language barriers were immense. If companies failed to uphold commitments, local courts could not be relied on for support. The World Bank only took direct stakes in companies, rather than buying shares on the stock market. So even if there were opportunities for growth in the Third World, it was not worthwhile for big fund managers in the West to search them out.

Another problem van Agtmael needed to address was simple image or "branding." After 1982, nobody wanted to invest in LDCs. The answer, reasoned van Agtmael, was to set up a fund. He and his colleagues would do the hard work and investors would have a shot at big gains. Portfolio diversification, or "safety in numbers," would help. Invest in many countries, and the risks posed by political or legal upheaval in any one of them diminished. He proposed to call this the Third World Equity Fund.

Van Agtmael's colleagues told him this was a terrible name. Then, "a light bulb went off in my brain," says van Agtmael. "Who wants to invest in the Third World? They weren't even second-rate; they were third-rate. That's when I came up with 'emerging markets,' which I felt had a little more pizzazz."[4] The name suggested "progress, uplift, and dynamism"[5] rather than the stagnation that went with the "Third World." In short, he wanted to rebrand a large swathe of the world and to create a new class of assets for investors to invest in. And he succeeded.

The transition from LDCs to emerging markets proved to be momentous. While the former tended to be in Latin America, now mired in its "lost decade," the latter would be associated more with the booming "tiger" economies of South East Asia. South Korea, arguably the greatest success story of the twentieth century, was completing its transition from a war-torn peasant nation into a modern, highly developed exporting powerhouse. It was even hosting the Olympics. Taiwan was close in its wake, followed by Thailand and Malaysia.

Van Agtmael and the World Bank did not have the field to themselves for long. As the model worked, others soon entered the market. Their job became easier, and the definition of "emerging market" became clearer after Morgan Stanley Capital International (now MSCI Barra) started its emerging markets index at the beginning of 1988. This made managers feel safer by giving them an index to group around. Like other indices, the MSCI soon outgrew its status as a passive benchmark to become an active guide to their investing.

Investing in that index proved to be mighty profitable. The MSCI index started on New Year's Day 1988 at 100. By November 1994, it stood at 563—staggering growth that attracted money from all sides. Initially, its correlation with the MSCI World index, covering the world's developed markets, was minimal. It even briefly went negative in 1989, suggesting that emerging markets provided a true hedge against events elsewhere in the world.[6]

But as more and more investors bought into emerging markets, their money began to drive them. If investors were feeling optimistic, then emerging markets allowed them to take more risk with the chance of bigger returns. If they were pessimistic, risky emerging markets stocks would be the first they sold. Over time, MSCI's emerging markets index correlated ever more closely with the developed world. By 2009, as Figure 6.1 shows, most of its daily movements could be explained by changes in the World index. Investors could easily expose themselves to the volatility of emerging markets. But it was perhaps more concerning that those emerging markets were now exposed to the volatile behavior of western investors.

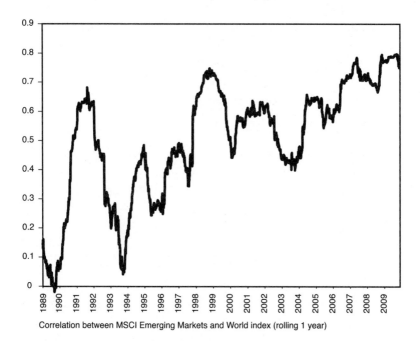

Correlation between MSCI Emerging Markets and World index (rolling 1 year)

Figure 6.1 *Emerging markets: ever more in sync*

45

The benchmark helped ensure that very disparate markets rose together. South Korea and Hungary, for example, have few things in common (and neither has much in common with Estonia), but gradually they and all other emerging countries started to move in unison (see Figure 6.2). Booming regions would help attract funds to regions that were in difficulties.

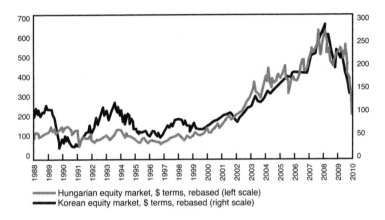

Figure 6.2 *Hungary and Korea—separated at birth?*

But the growth of the emerging markets was a classic example of how financial engineering led to lasting changes in the real economy. Similar financial engineering in the U.S. credit markets would soon have impacts just as profound.

In Summary

- Emerging markets funds made it easy for western investors to invest in the Third World, and they did. As they did so, once uncorrelated emerging markets started to move in alignment with the developed world and with each other.

- They were driven by commodity prices and the U.S. credit market—all forces for synchronized moves. And they were prone to sudden withdrawals of western capital.

Chapter 7

Junk Bonds

Junk bonds and securitized mortgages took from bankers the businesses of lending to risky companies and mortgage lending, and gave them to the markets. This drove a wedge between those who bear the risk of a loan and those who decide to make the loan, and encourages risk-taking. As a result, mortgage rates moved in line with other markets, cresting and crashing in unison with them.

The most widely recognized investor of the 1980s was not a businessman at all, but the actor Michael Douglas. As the fictional arbitrageur Gordon Gekko, his "greed is good" speech in the 1987 movie *Wall Street* summed up an era of excess in finance that resonated in popular culture. The era seemed to end with the disgrace of key financiers and the recession of 1990—but its innovations proved durable and are still central to the market drama two decades later.

Greed always drives Wall Street. What made Wall Streeters wealthier in the 1980s was something more prosaic: financial engineering. The taming of inflation led to lower and steadier interest rates, spurring financial innovations. Academic theories spurred investors to diversify into new kinds of assets. And deregulation allowed markets to peel off yet more business from banks, who hurried into new investments.

The most important breakthrough came in 1984 when the Reagan administration allowed banks to package mortgage loans into bonds and sell them to investors. This created a liquid market where mortgages could be traded, and moved power over housing finance into the markets. Until then, mortgage-lending still discernibly followed the model set in Victorian Britain, where it was built around "building societies"—mutual organizations that took in savings and made loans they monitored carefully, collecting mortgage repayments from door to door. This was inefficient and costly, but minimized defaults. Country after country, from the United States with its "Savings and Loans," to Spain in the 1970s, to Mexico in the 2000s, funded its emerging middle class this way.

Enter Wall Street. A mortgage is a clearly written financial contract, in which the borrower undertakes to make a certain flow of cash payments. The right to receive these payments can be sold to someone else (along with the risk that the homeowner defaults or repays in full ahead of schedule). If you put together enough mortgages, diversification comes to the rescue of due diligence. Broad statistical patterns help to predict the default rate, along with moves in the economy that most investors already spend much time trying to predict. The guiding principle, yet again, is "safety in numbers." Scrutinizing each borrower is impossible, but if you own enough mortgages, so the theory goes, it is not necessary either.

Once politicians gave them the go-ahead, investment banks started buying large blocks of mortgages from mortgage-lenders, many of whom were struggling with the high rates of the Volcker years, packaged them together, and used them to back bonds. Buyers of the bonds would receive the interest payments paid by the ultimate borrowers. As mortgage payments tend to be secure, the deal made sense for them—a slightly higher return than they could get on a treasury bond, in return for slightly greater risks.

Fannie Mae and Freddie Mac, the former Federal National Mortgage Association and Federal Home Loan Mortgage Corporation, were pivotal players. Fannie was formed during the New Deal as a government mortgage bank, charged with stimulating the housing market, but President Lyndon Johnson sold it off in 1968 in an unsuccessful attempt to keep the federal budget in balance. Despite being a quoted company, whose managers needed to make a profit for shareholders, it continued to be a "government-sponsored" entity—meaning, as far as many were concerned, that it still had an implicit guarantee if anything went wrong with its mortgages. When they took on mortgage bonds and sold them on the market, therefore, traders assumed that those bonds carried the federal government's guarantee. The proposition here was a slightly higher return than a treasury bond, and *no* extra risk. That meant Fannie and Freddie had to pay less interest on bonds and could therefore bid more to buy up mortgages from others, propelling the market. The ambiguous implicit guarantee helped to encourage Fannie and Freddie's managers, and their investors, to take excessive risks.

The presence of Fannie and Freddie in the market had unforeseen consequences. As lenders found it hard to compete with them, they would look in areas where Fannie and Freddie could not go, such as "jumbo" mortgages too expensive to qualify for federal help, and subprime mortgages for people with bad credit histories.

As a result of the innovation, the risks of default were no longer born by those who decided to make the loan in the first place. Instead, the lending officer who made the loan could sell the risk to someone else. Principals had once again been separated from agents.

The investment bankers who acted as agents did not always take their responsibilities wholly seriously, a process immortalized by

Michael Lewis' tell-all *Liar's Poker*,[1] probably the most entertaining book on finance ever written. In it, Lewis told the story of his years as a salesman at Salomon Brothers, the firm that led the mortgage-backed market, where mortgage traders would raucously gamble with each other throughout the day. Investment bankers grew obscenely rich. The banks that originated the loans also gained from securitization, as this took mortgages and their attendant risks off their balance sheets. They would take the money generated from selling the loans, and move on to something else.

The idea spread to the UK and much later to continental Europe, where there was less need for securitization as borrowers were more conservative and banks tended to be stronger. Critically, the technology worked as intended. It made it easier to finance mortgages and to spread risks, helping people buy their homes. But with the splitting of principals from agents, there was the risk that swings between greed and fear could change the affordability of buying houses—a profound building block of the economy.

Banks also lost control of another key function, lending to small or risky businesses, thanks to another market innovation: the junk bond. Like index funds, junk bonds (known officially as "high-yield bonds"), traced their origin to an entrepreneurial financier armed with academic research.

Michael Milken, of the investment bank Drexel Burnham Lambert, got the idea for junk bonds while studying economics as an undergraduate. He read a paper by Walter Braddock Hickman,[2] an academic who later became a Federal Reserve governor, which showed that from 1900 to 1943, a diversified portfolio of low-grade corporate bonds out-performed higher-quality blue-chip bonds, without greater risk. A subsequent study for the years of 1945 to 1965 came to the same conclusion.

The key was diversification, or another form of "safety in numbers." Buy enough different low-grade bonds, which must pay a higher rate of interest to persuade investors to buy them, and enough of them survive without default to leave the investor better off than in blue-chip bonds, which pay less interest. As with investing in emerging markets, risky investments that normally require a prohibitive amount of research can be palatable if financiers package enough of them together.

There was a flaw in the theory. Before the war, low-grade bonds were an unusual phenomenon. Generally, they had been issued by companies which had strong credit at the time, only later to fall on hard times. Rather than being regarded as an asset class, they were created by accident, but buying them at their lowest ebb worked out in the long run. It was not clear that the same would hold true of large amounts of bonds from companies that had bad credit at the time they issued them.

Nevertheless, Milken saw the opportunity. Persuade enough high-risk companies to issue debt, and investors could more easily be persuaded to enter the market in search of higher yields. Persuade enough investors to take the plunge into junk, and companies would be encouraged to issue. Once a market had been established, it would be easier for them to raise finance, improving smaller companies' overall prospects.

It worked, and Milken became the wealthiest financier on Wall Street. "Junk" bonds democratized markets. Demand for them grew so great that they became offensive weapons, as companies used high-yield bonds to make acquisitions that the market would not previously have been prepared to finance. Arguably such forces lay behind *Barbarians at the Gate*, the closest approach financial journalism has yet made to a Dickens novel,[3] which told the story of how the food-and-tobacco conglomerate RJR Nabisco was bought by a consortium of investors for $25 billion in a deal financed by high-yield debt. More than two decades later, it remains the most expensive buy-out of any company. RJR was hobbled by the huge interest payments it took on, but the deal made many financiers richer.

Junk bonds also won away yet another function from banks. Traditionally, loans to high-risk companies were made by bankers who could get close to the companies, talk to the managers, tour the premises, and act almost as low-grade consultants. Now, rather than do homework on the risks they were taking, investors could buy a range of bonds, and safety in numbers would see them through—some bonds would default, but most would survive. Yet again, a sensible insight from academia convinced investors that they had tamed risk.

Displaced bankers even fueled the demand for junk bonds. Savings and Loans, U.S. mortgage lenders, had plentiful cheap finance from deposits but found it hard to put the money to good use because other mortgage lenders, financed by the capital markets, could undercut them. Wall Street salesmen had the answer. They started selling them high-yield bonds which, at least in theory, should behave a lot like mortgages.

Several critical elements for the disaster of 2007–2008 were therefore in place. Prices in several sectors of the economy were now entrusted to the market, not bankers. Banks were at even more of a loose end. Junk credit could be traded. Mortgages could be traded. All that remained was to put the two together, and trade junk mortgages.

The market survived, even though the problems with junk bonds soon grew apparent. As several highly leveraged companies admitted they could not meet the huge interest payments they had taken on, junk bond prices tumbled by 11 percent in 1989. At the decade's end, Lipper Analytical Services reported money invested in junk-bond funds had grown by 145 percent since 1980. This sounded good but was worse than the 202 percent earned by investment-grade corporate bonds, or even the 177 percent made by virtually riskless U.S. treasury bonds. Almost one quarter of companies for which Drexel had issued junk bonds from 1977 onward defaulted by 1990—an exceptionally high failure rate.[4] This contributed to a horrible crisis for the Savings and Loans, many of whom turned out to be guilty of fraud, and they required a big government bailout in the recession of the early 1990s.

Milken himself went to prison, successfully battled cancer, and enjoyed a renaissance as a philanthropist. The story of his rise and fall even became the subject for an experimental ballet. But the American excess of the 1980s had nothing on the speculative madness that took over Japan at the same time. And Japan's crash, perversely, was to offer Americans a plentiful new source of cheap money.

In Summary

Junk bonds and securitized mortgages:

- Continued the decline of banks and the rise of markets.
- Split principals from agents.
- Gave lenders an incentive to take risks.
- Made financing far easier to find.
- Tied in the interest rate on mortgages more closely with other markets.

Chapter 8

The Carry Trade

> *"What we may be witnessing is not just the end of the Cold War or the passing of a particular period of post-war history, but the end of history as such: that is, the end point of mankind's ideological evolution and the universalization of western liberal democracy as the final form of human government."*
>
> Francis Fukuyama, 1990

The "carry trade" creates cheap money by borrowing in a currency with low interest rates, putting money into currencies with high interest rates, and pocketing the difference. Japan's market crash in 1990 brought low rates in its wake and created a great carry trade—and in 2009, investors borrowed U.S. dollars in another carry trade after the crash in the United States. The cheap money inflates bubbles. Once investors use it to fund investments in stocks, those markets rise and fall in line with the yen's exchange rate.

Japan loves to celebrate the New Year with performances of Beethoven's Ninth Symphony. On the night the 1980s ended, the Ode to Joy seemed appropriate. The world had just watched the Berlin Wall fall and communism subside across the Eastern European Bloc, soon to provide capitalism with a swathe of new emerging markets.

Months earlier in China, student demonstrations ended in a massacre in Beijing's Tiananmen Square. That crisis forced the country's supreme leader Deng Xiaoping to offer his people a new deal: The government would guarantee them economic growth in exchange for continued lack of democracy. That growth would come through capitalism red in tooth and claw and in 1990 China reopened the Shanghai Stock Exchange, which had been shuttered since it was closed by communist rebels in 1947.

These events changed the face of capitalism. But Japan administered an even greater shock. At the time the world's biggest stock market, it was caught in a bubble that peaked on New Year's Eve 1989. The international effects of the loss of wealth that resulted could easily have been as severe as the banking crises and depressions that followed Wall Street's Great Crash of 1929. But instead, as Japan fought the crisis, it turned its currency into a source of cheap funds for the rest of the world. What is now known as the "yen carry trade" would in time help bubbles to form in assets across the globe.

It is hard to exaggerate either the insanity of the bubble in Japan or the severity of what followed. In 1989, it briefly accounted for more than half of the world's entire stock market valuation,[1] even though its economy, about one-third of the size of the United States, accounted for only 8 percent of the world's gross domestic product. This was insane. Land and real estate prices were even more blatantly overvalued. At one point, the land on which the imperial palace is built in Tokyo was worth more than all the land in California.[2] Financial liberalization in the 1980s, making it easier to raise mortgages, and encouraging foreign investment, fed the bubble.

From 1985 to 1989, the Nikkei 225, Japan's main stock index, quadrupled—and over the next five years it lost more than 80 percent. It has never staged a lasting recovery. At the end of 2009 it was oscillating around the level of 10,000 that it first reached in 1985. At its peak it was nearly 40,000.

The bubble had burst under its own weight. Houses grew so expensive as to threaten social unrest, and when the government tried to rein in mortgage-lending, borrowers defaulted, land prices dropped, and stock prices fell with them. In essence, it was a repeat of the Mexican crisis—intense capital flows and excessive lending led to a bubble and over-extended banks. The critical difference was that Japan was much bigger than Mexico.

As in Mexico, banks were points of weakness. Many mortgages extended at the mania's height would never be repaid. If Japan's banks admitted that and marked down their assets accordingly, then substantially the entire banking system would be bankrupt. So regulators did not force the issue and the banks limped on, unable to stimulate the economy, while Japan lapsed into outright deflation—falling price levels—as the money dried up.

The key for international investors lay in the government's response, which was to cut rates in an attempt to get money flowing once more. On New Year's Eve 1989, the Bank of Japan's target lending rate stood at 4.25 percent. Then came a long and steady dive as activity stagnated and repeated doses of cheap money failed to stimulate the economy or the banks back into life. By 1995, the discount rate fell to 0.5 percent. In 2001, it reached 0.1 percent and stayed there. Figure 8.1 shows how activity dried up.

This did not happen in a vacuum. Such low interest rates weakened the yen and made it maddeningly difficult for Japanese people to save money. That created an opportunity for international traders with access to the foreign exchange market, which came to be known as the "yen carry trade." This is perhaps the most controversial and least visible aspect of the global bubble. "Carry" is traders' jargon for the cost of holding a security. For example, holding a gold bar costs money, because the storage is very expensive. But borrowing in yen is almost costless—from the late 1990s, that cost was only the minimal interest rate charged on Japanese accounts.

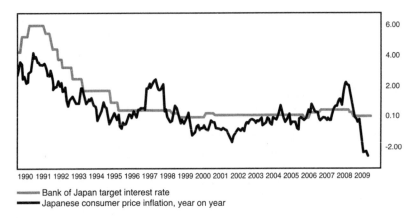

1990 1991 1992 1993 1994 1995 1996 1997 1998 1999 2000 2001 2002 2003 2004 2005 2006 2007 2008 2009

▬▬ Bank of Japan target interest rate
▬▬ Japanese consumer price inflation, year on year

Figure 8.1   *After the crash: cheap money and deflation*

Higher interest rates tend to strengthen a currency. If the UK raises rates while the United States does not, for example, that should attract funds out of dollars into pounds, because the pound has become a more attractive place to park money. That flow of money will strengthen the pound. Hence low rates tend to lead to persistently weak currencies. And that opens up the possibility of a great "carry trade"—borrow in yen, put the money into a currency with higher rates, and pocket the difference, or "carry." Providing the yen does not suddenly rise, making it more expensive to repay the loan, this is very easy money that can be put toward opportunities elsewhere.

Markets' self-fulfilling nature takes a role. The more investors attempt to operate a carry trade, the safer a bet it will be because the flows of money out of Japan that they create will weaken the yen. But if volatility rises, or investors get nervous, they will take their profits from the carry trade and strengthen the yen in the process. While this trade worked beautifully for most of the time, it was an intrinsically dangerous way to raise money, with the risk that a spike in volatility could send all traders' calculations awry. This meant that for the years of Japan's malaise, its currency moved on the animal spirits of traders around the world, rather than on any factors endemic to the Japanese economy.

Who exactly practiced this carry trade remains a subject of passionate debate. It eludes precise measurement. "Mrs. Watanabe"—the popular tag for the typical Japanese retail investor—is a plausible candidate. She could make no money on domestic bank accounts, or in the local stock market, but could profit from the artificially cheapening currency by investing elsewhere. The more Japanese investors entrusted their savings overseas, the more the yen weakened. This weakening itself made Mrs. Watanabe richer and encouraged her friends to do the same thing. A new category of savings products arose as "Uridashi" bonds offered Japanese investors returns denominated in New Zealand or Australian dollars, or South African rands—all currencies with far higher interest rates.

But it was not just Mrs. Watanabe. International traders also made money by carry trading. That can be seen by the way the yen would spike within minutes in response to a shift in the global appetite for risk—a speed beyond Mrs. Watanabe's reach. And Mrs. Watanabe had nothing to do with the extension of the carry trade to other currencies such as the U.S. dollar and Swiss franc in the next decade, which was prompted by falling interest rates in other big economies.

After the Federal Reserve cut rates as low as 1 percent in the aftermath of the 9/11 terrorist attacks of 2001, the Bank of International Settlements (BIS) found that many traders started borrowing in dollars as part of carry trades.[3] The Swiss franc, another currency with low rates, had the same phenomenon. Hungarians, freed from communism, often chose to take out mortgages denominated in Swiss francs. This gave them a low interest rate and freed them to invest elsewhere, but also exposed them to potential disaster if their own currency, the forint, should fall. In the 18 months leading up to January 2007, Hungarians borrowed about 3.25 billion Swiss francs

($2.6 billion at the time) for home mortgages, while the total stock of Swiss franc loans in Hungary reached about 7.5 percent of Hungary's GDP at the time.[4] Destination currencies for carry traders enjoyed phenomenal growth. According to the BIS, turnover in the Australian dollar rose by 150 percent between 2001 and 2004—a period in which Australian rates rose as U.S. dollar rates fell, and the Australian dollar gained strongly. This was driven by online technology, which made it easier to trade in these markets by increasing use of the carry trade.

Japan's implosion thus redirected big money flows. They found a home in freshly emerging countries, inflated bubbles there, and also helped to inflate a synchronized super-bubble by providing a cheap but unstable source of funds for the whole world. As the practice took hold, it distorted the world economy and the terms of global trade by making some currencies undervalued and others overvalued. As Figure 8.2 shows, in the period from 2003 to 2009, the carry trade exchange rate of the Australian dollar against the yen was almost perfectly correlated with the U.S. S&P 500 stock index—a bizarre outcome that showed both markets were inefficiently priced.

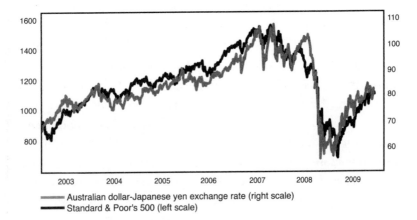

Australian dollar-Japanese yen exchange rate (right scale)
Standard & Poor's 500 (left scale)

Figure 8.2 *Perverse correlations: U.S. stocks and the carry trade*

History had not ended in 1990. But the yen carry trade was not the only example of how investors could make money out of foreign exchange in a post-gold standard world. As the 1990s progressed, foreign exchange became an asset class in its own right.

In Summary

- The bursting of Japan's bubble did not create crises elsewhere thanks to the emergence of new markets and to the carry trade, which effectively allowed global investors to enjoy low Japanese rates.
- The carry trade created extra funds for speculation and led to tight correlations between the value of the yen and then the dollar and stock markets. It is a bet on low volatility.

Chapter 9

Foreign Exchange

"Today has been an extremely difficult and turbulent day."
British Chancellor Norman Lamont, Wednesday,
September 16, 1992

Foreign exchange is supposed to be a series of zero-sum games that creates no value. But a series of currency coups in the 1990s prompted investors to treat it as its own asset class. Stock and bond investors played the currency markets and exchange rates started to synchronize with stock markets.

As the City of London started trading on Wednesday, September 16, 1992, it was hit by dramatic news. The Bank of England, not then independent of the government, had raised its base rate by 2 percentage points, from 10 percent to 12 percent. It set in motion a day that proved beyond doubt that markets, not governments, set exchange rates—and convinced many mainstream investors to start playing in the foreign exchange market, a decision that led markets to move ever more in alignment.

Most British homeowners had variable-rate mortgages, and the country was in the grips of a real estate slump. The Bank's move meant that monthly mortgage payments would instantly go up by 20 percent. It also implied that the government was deadly serious about defending the value of the pound sterling, which for two years had been part of the exchange rate mechanism of the European Monetary

System, an agreement to keep Europe's main currencies trading within a broad band of each other. A drastic interest rate rise was a way to maintain the pound's value.

The pound continued to fall.

At 2:00 p.m., the few City financiers who had found the time to go to lunch got back to their offices to find that the Bank was raising rates again, this time by 3 percentage points, to 15 percent. By extension, the government was so determined to defend the pound that it was ready to raise homeowners' borrowing costs by 50 percent in one day. Nobody believed it. The pound kept falling, even as the Treasury bought pounds with its currency reserves in an attempt to bolster it.

That night, Norman Lamont, the chancellor, announced he was "suspending" sterling's membership of the exchange rate mechanism. It never rejoined. The pound dropped about 10 percent against the dollar within hours and the next day, he cut British interest rates to nine percent.

The incident went down in British political history as "Black Wednesday," and sentenced the ruling Conservative party to more than a decade in opposition. Global investors were more intrigued to find out exactly how it had happened. Later that month, *The Times* of London talked to George Soros, a big international investor. He admitted that his funds had made a $950 million profit from the fall of the pound and as much again from other currency bets during the chaos surrounding the exchange rate mechanism.[1]

Having studied the economic situation, he believed that the British could not keep the pound within the necessary band against the Deutsche Mark. The UK economy was in recession and he did not see the German government helping out by lowering interest rates. He also decided that any move to bet against the pound must be done with overwhelming force, so that his move could become a self-fulfilling prophecy.

Soros told *The Times* he had bet $10 billion, after negotiating lines of credit with dozens of banks in advance. He took the Bank's rise to 12 percent as the signal that sterling was about to crack, so he borrowed the maximum that he could in pounds, and used it all to buy Deutsche Marks. This forced the pound down. Once sterling had dropped by 10 percent, Soros converted his Marks back into pounds, and made a 10 percent profit.

These details made him sound to British ears like a villain in a James Bond film. To investors, however, they showed that there were opportunities in foreign exchange (known as "forex"). Maybe forex might even be an asset class in its own right.

There are strong arguments against this. Unlike stocks or bonds, forex cannot grow over time. Every forex trade has a winner and an equal and opposite loser. If you sell dollars for euros and the euro gains, then you win; and whoever bought your dollars loses exactly as much as you won. To this extent, every trade is a "zero-sum game," in which the sum of the winnings and losses of the various traders is always zero. The total worth of shares can rise from year to year, if companies trade profitably. The sum value generated in the forex market each year should be zero. While Bretton Woods was in force, and rates were pegged to gold, the opportunities were in any case very limited.

But reality is more complex. Forex is the biggest and most liquid market that exists. Every day, some $3.2 trillion moves between currencies. Many of these bets are not placed by investors. Instead they are placed by tourists, or importers or exporters who receive payments in a foreign currency. These people are generally dealing out of necessity, and they are not trying to predict trends in the forex market. Thus, forex is a series of zero-sum games, in which many of the competitors are not trying to win, or are forced to play at a time when they are likely to lose. Thus forex begins to look like an interesting investment opportunity.

In the 1990s, it also had the advantage that it was not correlated with stocks, so it offered the opportunity to diversify risk. And the fallout from the end of the Bretton Woods system had created other opportunities. The Chicago Mercantile Exchange started trading foreign exchange futures contracts in 1972. These allowed companies to fix an exchange rate for transactions in the future, and thus helped them hedge their risks—but they also made it easier for a speculator to make a straightforward bet on future moves in exchange rates.

And so funds and big investment institutions started to devote money exclusively to playing foreign exchange. The intervention of governments added to the possibilities, after Soros established that artificially set exchange rates simply could not last if investors decided against them. Currencies would have to float truly freely and create ever more interesting opportunities for foreign exchange speculation in the process.

In 1994, another pegged exchange rate came under pressure and buckled. This time it was a familiar victim: Mexico. The cause was the same ruthless dynamic that had played out in the LDCs crisis and again in Japan. Money had poured in to Mexico during the emerging markets boom. Its banks, freshly privatized once more, were indulging in an ill-advised lending binge. Then Alan Greenspan, who took over from Paul Volcker at the Federal Reserve in 1987, decided to rein in markets, which had been rallying since 1990. He raised rates, forcing serious losses on bond investors.

This hurt Mexico because higher rates pushed the dollar upward. After suffering the Zapatista Rebellion and the murder of a presidential candidate early in the year, Mexico was losing credibility and spending its foreign reserves swiftly as it tried to keep the peso within self-imposed limits. In December, a new government came to power under President Ernesto Zedillo. It had not had the chance to build up credibility on world markets and decided to widen the peg at which the peso traded against the dollar.

But when the new finance minister, Jaime Serra Puche, announced on December 20 that the peso would now be allowed to depreciate by 15 percent, it caused turmoil. He had to let the peso float freely two days later, and it soon dropped by more than 50 percent. The luckless Serra Puche resigned less than a month into his tenure.

The peso itself had only been slightly overvalued ahead of the move. But what looked like a speculative assault proved to have been an almost accidental attack. Earlier in 1994, the Mexican government started issuing bonds to foreigners that were payable in pesos but indexed to the dollar, known as *tesobonos*. If the peso weakened, the amount payable to the foreign banks who had bought the *tesobonos* would increase to stay constant in dollar terms. It thus reassured them about the risk of devaluation—but carried the risk that Mexico might have to find more pesos.

However, unknown to regulators, virtually all $16 billion in *tesobonos* that were issued were then swapped back to Mexican banks, who instead guaranteed to pay the U.S. banks much the same interest rate that they would receive from a dollar account. If Mexico had avoided a currency crisis, the banks would have done well, because the *tesobonos* had a high interest rate. But once the peso started to fall, they owed more to the U.S. banks, who started to demand their money. To provide it to them, the Mexican banks had to sell pesos and buy dollars, pushing the peso down further.[2]

A devaluation that looked as though it would cause a problem for banks in New York instead caused a cataclysm for banks in Mexico City. By the time the crisis was over, more than half of all Mexican bank assets had been wiped out, more than 90 percent of the Mexican banking system was in foreign hands, and a cascading "Tequila Crisis" tipped over into crises throughout Latin America.

The incident showed how interconnected markets had become. Raising rates in the United States had big effects elsewhere, while modern international financial flows made it hard to tell exactly where those effects would be felt. It also intensified the rush by institutions to invest in foreign exchange. The Tequila Crisis was an ugly moment for world markets, but anyone who had bet on a fall in the peso, alongside their investment in stocks and bonds, would have felt much more comfortable.

Investing in forex as an asset class peaked in the years leading up to the crisis of 2007. According to the BIS, total forex daily turnover in 2007 averaged $3.2 trillion—quadruple its level in 1992 when Soros made his attack on the pound.[3] Of this, 40 percent came from non-bank financial groups—largely investment funds treating forex as an investment. A decade earlier, such trade had only accounted for 20 percent of forex volumes. Therefore, trading in forex had become vastly greater, and most of the increase came from new investors treating forex as its own asset class.

This was a powerful synchronizing force for markets. A fund manager who liked the prospects for economic growth in Brazil, for example, would buy both the Brazilian currency (the real), and Brazilian stocks. Both actions pushed up the real and encouraged more investors to get involved. This made much of the world doubly vulnerable to swings in sentiment by international investors—but luckily for them, investors in the United States were consistently, or even irrationally, exuberant.

In Summary

- Foreign exchange is now a game for markets, subject to the same herding tendency that marks the stock market.

- Because many traders in the market do not aim to make profits, forex investment may be a profitable investment strategy—but in practice it merely amplifies flows of funds driven by equities and commodities.

- Most investors should not touch forex as an investment in its own right, at least while it stays correlated to equities.

Chapter 10

Irrational Exuberance

> *"How do we know when irrational exuberance has unduly escalated asset values, which then become subject to unexpected and prolonged contractions as they have in Japan over the past decade?"*
>
> Alan Greenspan, December 5, 1996

Baby boomers piled into mutual funds, inflating share prices and prompting fund managers to crowd into hot stocks. The 1997 Asia Crisis showed that they had become the world's investors of last resort. It prompted China and other Asian countries to build up stockpiles of dollars. That lowered U.S. interest rates and allowed more bubbles to form.

When they have credibility, central bankers can move markets easily. Just asking one hypothetical question will do it. That is what happened on December 6, 1996, after Alan Greenspan asked the question that opens this chapter. It was buried deep in a long and often turgid speech, and he offered no answer, but the mere fact that he raised the question caused a fright. It implied that the level of asset prices itself worried him, and that he might raise rates to stop a bubble from forming. He rammed home his message by provocatively comparing the United States to Japan.

European stock markets fell by more than 4 percent within hours, the sharpest fall in several years.[1] Greenspan proved deadly earnest.

A few months later, with U.S. stocks back to setting new highs, Greenspan followed through, raised lending rates, and successfully engineered a 10 percent "correction" in U.S. stocks. But they did not stay down for long and soon surged upward once more. Greenspan had correctly diagnosed a deep-seated case of exuberance, but arguably, its roots were not irrational. By 1996, the post-war baby boomers were entering their 50s. Retirement was a fast-approaching reality and they needed to bolster their savings. Stocks had risen every year but one since Volcker brought inflation under control in 1982, so it was not surprising that boomers thought they were the best bet.

The ERISA reform of pensions in the 1970s had shifted the onus for deciding where to invest from paternalistic pension funds, which guarantee a proportion of their final salary as a pension, to individuals themselves. Institutions would have maintained a relatively conservative allocation to bonds. But individuals were given an ever broader choice of funds to invest in—ranging across the United States into international stocks. Many were making up for lost time after not saving much earlier, so they poured into the stock market. If there was a sell-off, all seemed to believe, the smart thing was to "buy on the dips."

The Internet, an exciting new technology at the time, made playing the market much easier. Small investors could place money and switch it between funds with the click of a mouse. Generally, they put their money wherever the profits had just been. In the first nine months of 1997, immediately following the irrational exuberance speech, retail investors poured $177 billion into mutual funds. This helped complete the institutionalization of investment, with funds holding $2.4 trillion in stocks, a tenfold increase since the October 1987 Black Monday crash a decade earlier. Indeed, fund managers were increasingly alarmed by the money coming in their direction, which it was ever more difficult to invest sensibly.

Jack Bogle's firm Vanguard was out-selling all others but was not happy about it. "We are very worried," a spokesman said after record sales early in 1997. "We really are trying to put a damper on these numbers because we fear it is just going to add to the engines on this stock-market bandwagon, and more people are going to want to jump on. The last thing you want to do is throw yourself on to a speeding bandwagon."[2]

Arthur Levitt, then the chief regulator of share trading as the head of the U.S. Securities and Exchange Commission, also sounded the alarm. "Investors are not as informed as they should be," he said. "This is especially troubling because most of these new investors have experienced only a bull market. I fear that in a downturn those who don't understand risk may react precipitously and carelessly, at great cost to themselves and our markets." In other words, money that had hurried into the stock market could hurry out again at the first sign of trouble.

Irrational exuberance had its great test on October 27 that year. Its roots lay in a crisis on the other side of the world, for the "tiger" economies of South East Asia. After the Japanese bubble burst, Japan's companies had started investing in their near neighbors. Western investors did the same. In the first half of the decade, share prices in Thailand, Malaysia, and Indonesia, the developing fringe of the region, rose by between 300 and 500 percent.[3]

The region could not use the money. Its period of explosive growth almost over, its profits were stagnant. In South Korea, the region's leader, half of the 30 biggest conglomerates made a loss in 1996.[4] Instead of finding a productive home, the money pushed real estate prices into a bubble. Once those prices began to fall, the banks who financed them suffered crippling losses. When international investors sensed that Thai banks had a problem, flows of foreign capital went into reverse.

Underlying weaknesses were revealed once the region's over-valued exchange rates came under attack, as investors pulled money out. With their currencies falling, the cost of repaying debts, mostly denominated in dollars, quickly became unbearable. In this situation, governments can only defend themselves if they have big reserves of foreign currency, which they can then sell to push up their own currency. Lacking such reserves, the governments of first Thailand, then Malaysia, Indonesia, and South Korea succumbed to devaluations—and faced up to repaying their piles of outstanding dollar-denominated debt.

Western markets nervously held firm as the Asian "contagion" spread across the Pacific Rim, but it could not last. On October 27, Hong Kong, the region's biggest financial center, with a currency tied to the U.S. dollar, capitulated. Its stocks fell seven percent, provoking a day of reckoning in New York and London.

Selling started early, and intensified as the day drew on. Shortly after lunchtime in Wall Street, the Dow Jones Industrial Average had fallen 350 points, triggering for the first time the "circuit-breaker" rule the New York Stock Exchange had adopted in the wake of Black Monday ten years earlier. This mandated that trading should stop for 30 minutes. The idea was to get everyone to calm down. It had the opposite effect. Unnerved by the fact that trading had been halted, many traders pushed the button to "sell" as soon as trading restarted. Within minutes the Dow had fallen another 200 points, and the circuit-breakers forced the exchange to close almost an hour early, after the worst day for U.S. stocks in a decade. If the selling carried on the next day and turned into a rout, then a true global financial disaster seemed possible. How, Wall Streeters worried that evening, would the new army of retail investors react? Would they sell?

They need not have worried. Small investors were already buying. Overnight orders to buy stock placed with Charles Schwab, the biggest discount broker in the United States, outnumbered "sell" orders three to one—even as stock markets in Asia and Europe sold off in response to the events in New York. Once the day began, the volume of orders only intensified, with Schwab's total volume running at three times its average. The same thing happened at all the big mutual funds.[5]

Panic on New York's trading floors gave way to something like euphoria as traders realized the buying power from small investors was pushing prices up. They joined in. From its bottom that day, the Dow rebounded by almost 5 percent, one of the best days on record. Small investors had come to the rescue; the worst fears of Arthur Levitt had not come to pass.

Overconfidence, the vital ingredient of any bubble, ratcheted up another notch. Anxious to take the temperature of its customers, Schwab surveyed 500 of its callers on Tuesday. A full 92 percent of them claimed to have expected a market correction—which raised the question why they had not sold ahead of it—while 81 percent planned to buy "more stocks at lower prices." With the market driven by investors who seemed certain that stocks, in the long run, were a one-way, upward bet, there was nowhere for stocks to go but up. Setting a sensible price for capital was impossible in such an environment.

The effect on institutions' behavior was insidious. "Career risk" flooded out all other considerations. Logically, the sensible action at this time was to invest in "value" stocks (those that look cheap relative to the value of the assets on their balance sheets), rather than run with the herd. But if managers wanted to hold on to their careers, they had to do the opposite, and this served only to magnify the overconfidence of their clients. Value investors lost their jobs, while mainstream fund managers piled into popular stocks.

Exuberance also created "career risk" for politicians. The total assets of mutual funds, now greater even than the total assets of banks, were frighteningly transparent. If the stock market took a tumble, savers (who were also voters) would know straight away. Politicians already disliked raising interest rates because it makes it harder for people to borrow, but now they had a new incentive to avoid pushing down the stock market.

America's baby boomers became the world's investors of last resort. It was their money, ultimately, that drove up the tiger economies in the first place and then brought them down, and it was their willingness to feed more capital into markets that allowed the Asian currency crises to be contained.

In Asia, perceptions were different and politicians had incentives to behave in a way that also, in time, inflated global asset bubbles. After their crisis, they endured years of slow growth. Determined to be able to defend their currencies in the future, they bought dollars. Rather than pegging their currencies, which merely invited speculation, they let them float—but built huge stockpiles of dollar-denominated assets, usually in the form of bonds issued by the U.S. Treasury or by Fannie Mae and Freddie Mac, that could be sold in defense if their currencies should ever come under attack again. By buying U.S. bonds they pushed down their yields, and hence reduced interest rates for Americans. That stoked the final stages of the credit bubble.

International interconnections were now stronger and more fateful than ever. In the late 1990s, the aging baby boom generation had come together with a newly institutionalized investment industry to create a stock market that was almost incapable of going down.

In Summary

- Irrational exuberance made U.S. retail investors the world's investor of last resort, pushing up prices across the world. That exuberance intimidated governments into trying to stop stock market falls and stoked moral hazard.

- It helped the world avoid a severe impact from the 1997 Asian crisis—but that crisis had the lasting legacy that Asian governments bought dollars and pushed down U.S. borrowing rates.

Chapter 11

Banks Too Big to Fail

> *"Any fool can make things bigger, more complex, and more violent. It takes a touch of genius—and a lot of courage—to move in the opposite direction."*
>
> Albert Einstein

Global mega-mergers left many banks "too big to fail"—so important to the economy that governments could not let them collapse. This created "moral hazard"—with no fear of failure, they had less incentive to avoid risks. Subsequent regulations gave banks further incentives to speculate—and as truly global institutions, they had an impact across the world.

It was an unholy Holy Week. On April 5, 1998, Palm Sunday, lawyers put the finishing touches to a merger that revolutionized finance. Citicorp, long the most truly international bank, was to merge with Travelers Group, a sprawling mélange of financial services companies pieced together by the entrepreneur Sandy Weill that included big investment banks, consumer credit companies, and an insurer. The deal signaled the final abandonment of the post-Depression attempt to keep U.S. banks tightly regulated, and replaced it with an environment where banks were free to grow with impunity.

Weill and his Citicorp partner John Reed announced the deal under a hastily put together name and logo for the new entity—the word "Citigroup" sat under Travelers' umbrella logo. With total assets of almost $700 billion, bigger at the time than the gross domestic products of all but seven countries, this was a financial company on a scale previously undreamed of. But it was not just the size of the new Citigroup that caused a sensation. The new company, as constituted, was plainly illegal.

Under the Glass-Steagall Act, in force since 1934, a deposit-taking commercial bank could not sit under the same roof, or umbrella, as an insurer or an investment bank. Now Citibank would do both. Bankers had been finding ways around the Glass-Steagall Act for a while, with regulators often helping them find loopholes. It seemed anachronistic and put the United States out of step with the rest of the world. In Europe, for example, "bancassurance," with large banks offering insurance as part of a "one-stop shop" to their customers, was the norm. Weill now seemed confident he could end the Glass-Steagall Act once and for all.

In another political environment, Weill's confidence might have been taken for hubris, but in the late 1990s, no politician wanted to stand in the way of the stock market. Republicans in Congress soon thrashed out a deal with President Bill Clinton (whom they had tried to impeach only months earlier), the central Glass-Steagall provisions were struck down with only weak guidelines to replace them, and Weill joined the president at the ceremonial signing.

Citigroup's merger was only the first big deal of Holy Week in 1998. Over Good Friday weekend, two more massive banks were hatched. NationsBank, a regional bank based in Charlotte, North Carolina, took over BankAmerica, a huge Californian bank with operations around the world, for $66.6 billion, while First Chicago NBD, long the most powerful bank in the Midwest, sold itself to Bank One. These deals also showed that the post-Depression banking structure was over. For decades, U.S. banks were barred from doing business outside their home states, leading to the balkanization of the industry. In the 1980s, there were as many as 15,000 banks in the United States, many of them with only one branch. As the mega-mergers hit, there were still as many as 9,000. At this time, Britain and Canada, similar countries in many ways, had 212 and 53 banks, respectively. If the American banking system were to become as concentrated as Britain's, it would have, at the most, 1,000 banks; if it were as concentrated as Canada's, it would have just 500. With computers, bigger banks created economies of scale, and bankers argued that this would allow them to provide better value for clients.

But their scale raised the issue of what economists call "moral hazard." Banking regulation ultimately rests on capitalism's application of human fear to the actions of banks' managers: If they take too many risks, they should face the risk that the bank goes bust. But at some point when a bank grows big, its collapse would wreak so much damage on the economy that it could not be allowed to happen. There is no hard and fast measure of when this happens, but you know it when you see it: The new Bank of America was plainly too big to fail. Once a bank knows it cannot fail, it has no incentive to avoid excessive risks. This is moral hazard.

This unholy Holy Week thus forced the U.S. government to make fateful decisions—and the banks swiftly got what they wanted. Both big mergers, and several others, were waved through and completed within months.

Not only American banks felt the urge to merge. European banks also grew bigger and found footholds in the United States. With the Glass-Steagall Act repealed, they could swallow up Wall Street brokers, as when UBS bought Paine Webber in 2000. Because Wall Street was so important to them, this meant that the United States became the *de facto* regulator for all the world's biggest banks—as shown when U.S. regulators held up the merger of two giant Swiss banks, UBS and Swiss Banking Corporation, after revelations that they were still holding on to money deposited with them before the war by Holocaust victims.[1]

While America's conservative banking regulations had avoided the problem of banks becoming "too big to fail" for more than half a century, Europe already had this problem, which the splurge of deals as the U.S. finally relaxed its rules only intensified. By the time the crisis hit in 2007, the total bank assets in the United States were roughly equal to the GDP. In Iceland, which had the world's most overblown financial system, bank assets were 8.9 times the size of the economy, while for Switzerland the figure was 7.8. The UK's bank assets were 5 times the size of its economy, France's were 4 times, and even Germany's were almost 3 times. In these jurisdictions, large banks tended to be a source of national pride and income, and their growth had historically been encouraged.[2] The conservative regime in the United States had somewhat inhibited such excesses, but European banks now became not only too big to fail, but arguably also too big for their own governments to rescue.

Another trend also reached its completion. Aside from being separate from commercial banks, investment banks had been run as partnerships. The senior bankers, who made decisions on all the biggest deals, took a share of the profits and also stood to be liable for losses. This balanced fear and greed in their minds—in the event of a collapse, they stood to lose all that they had gained before.

But starting in the 1970s, Wall Street's partnerships decided to float on the market. On the other side of the Atlantic, many of the old London investment banks and brokers disappeared inside bigger public banks after the City of London's 1986 "Big Bang," which did away with old distinctions between stockbrokers and marketmakers.

Bankers still had an incentive to make profits through the bonus system. But they did not stand to lose what they had already gained in a collapse. That fate belonged to shareholders. As a banker could easily set himself up for life with a few good years on Wall Street, this significantly lowered fear in their calculations and aided greed.

In May 1999, a year after the Citigroup deal, Goldman Sachs, Wall Street's most prestigious and successful investment bank, finally took itself public. The firm had a cherished 130-year-old partnership culture, but it could now raise money from shareholders. Going public was an instant one-off boon for the men then in charge, several of whom played key roles once the crisis hit a decade later. At the price the bank offered shares, the stake of Hank Paulson, then the chief executive, was automatically worth $206 million.[3]

The move toward *laissez faire* from banking regulators came to its logical conclusion in 2004 with the Basel II Accord, named after the Swiss city that hosts the Bank of International Settlements. This body is a central bank for other central banks, lending money to the central banks that need it and coordinating banking regulations across borders. Basel II effectively gave the big U.S. and European banks all they wanted.

A key task of regulators is to set how much capital banks must put aside. The more capital they have, the more they can withstand losses from bad loans or bad trades. Banks might think they are engaged in low-risk activities, but if the regulator disagrees, they can be required to keep extra money in reserves. In Basel II, regulators put more emphasis on banks' own assessments of the risks that confronted them, even though they were now too big to fail. It unwittingly drove the ultimate credit crisis by requiring far fewer reserves against mortgage-backed securities or against securities with the top available credit rating of AAA—moves that prompted banks to buy mortgage-backed securities.[4]

A perverse consequence was to vest immense power in the rating agencies, such as Moody's, Standard & Poor's, and Fitch, who give debt offerings a rating before they are launched. The trick was to persuade the agencies to rate securities AAA. The danger in the new system came in the event of a downgrade from AAA, as even if the bonds or debts in question had still not defaulted, this would force banks to raise more capital to stay within the Basel II regulations.

Compared to the 1950s, the banking industry had changed utterly. It was now peopled by investment bankers betting with other people's (shareholders') money, not their own. Commercial bankers were divorced from the consequences of their decisions by the commercial paper market, mortgage securitization, and money market funds. Mutual funds, largely tied to the main indices, had taken their place as the main allocators of capital. But even though many of their businesses were no longer covered by deposit insurance, the bigger banks operated as though they had government protection.

Under economic rationality, commercial banks would have wound themselves down and closed as they lost their businesses. But with human nature governing them, executives did something different. The business of taking deposits in noninterest bearing accounts is a good one—from the banker's perspective, your clients are effectively lending you money for free. With the Glass-Steagall Act no longer in place, it was easier to put that money to work in the securities markets.

At the time, few sounded the alarm, but Henry Kaufman, a Wall Street economist known as Doctor Doom in the 1970s for his successful predictions of high interest rates, tried to spoil the party. In words that now sound prophetic, he warned that the new huge banks should be "treated more and more like public utilities" rather than entrepreneurially run private enterprises.[5]

For him, the problems managing the "new behemoth banking institutions" and the "fallout when the U.S. financial bubble bursts" posed latent threats to U.S. prosperity. At times in the years since, Citigroup and other big banks have indeed seemed too big and complex for anyone to manage. But he contended that the money in mutual funds had created a political imperative for the central bank to begin "acquiescing to increases in asset prices but taking policy measures to stop, or at least contain, asset price declines." His prediction came spectacularly true within months, taking moral hazard to a dangerous new level.

In Summary

- Mergers and the removal of post-Depression regulations created a group of big and complex international banks that were far too large for any government to allow them to fail.

- This created moral hazard—the tendency to take more risks when you know you have protection if something goes wrong.

- The loss of traditional businesses and new international reserves rules gave them extra incentives to expand into new and riskier markets—most blatantly subprime mortgages.

Chapter 12

Hedge Funds

"Note how easy it is to show a short-term profit in a financial institution: you have only to take on risk."
David Beim and Charles Calomiris of Columbia University

Loosely regulated hedge funds have many advantages: they can move freely among markets, they can profit from prices going down as well as up, and they can increase their returns by using borrowed money. The meltdown of Long-Term Capital Management (LTCM) in September 1998 showed that they compelled markets to move in alignment; its rescue stoked moral hazard.

If banks appear logically doomed to decline, the same logic points to the rise of hedge funds. LTCM was the biggest and most ambitious, but it has become the perfect exemplar of the hedge fund model's dangers. Its fall in 1998 cost its founders, including two Nobel laureate economists, some $1.9 billion of their personal wealth[1] and caused the world's biggest financial crisis since the war. Beyond its human drama, the episode demonstrated that hedge funds had the power to drive markets to move together. The response to its near-collapse was an easy money policy that was still having painful consequences a decade later.

The term "hedge fund" is a loose one. Any fund that does not obey the restrictions that regulators put on investments aimed at the general public, such as a mutual fund, is technically a hedge fund. In return for this permissive treatment, they are required not to advertise and may only take money from the very wealthy (generally those with at least $1 million to spare) who are investing money they can afford to lose. The advantages are enormous—they can keep their holdings confidential, they can charge more in fees, they can bet with borrowed money, and they can sell short.

As with mutual funds, the structure of hedge fund fees creates perverse incentives. The standard model is known in industry vernacular as "two and twenty"—managers get 2 percent of the assets they manage, plus 20 percent of the profits they make in any given year. The exact numbers vary, and the performance fee often only clicks in after the fund has beaten some predetermined threshold, but this still creates asymmetric incentives. If you come up with a way to win big in a given year, you take home a big chunk of the profits; if you lose big, you still keep your 2 percent management fee. This is a form of moral hazard. The incentive is to take big risks in return for good performance that will last at least until the end of the year. If hedge funds can latch on to a trend, therefore, they want to make that trend last longer (or possibly, to turn overpriced markets into bubbles). They have the tools to help this happen.

One big weapon is short-selling, a maneuver that profits from prices going down and hence inspires much animosity. A fund borrows a stock (generally from a big index fund that has to hold the stock and can benefit from the interest it charges on the loan) and then sells it. If its price falls, the short-seller can buy it back, return the stock to its owner, and pocket the difference in price. The ability to profit from downward moves helps manage risks, but also creates new ones. The gains from selling short are limited to 100 percent, while potential losses are infinite. Buy a stock at $10 and the most you can make is

$10 (if it goes bust). If it goes up, there is no limit on the amount you could lose. This is why regulators make it hard for mainstream firms to sell short.

The most important weapon is borrowed money, or leverage, which allows funds to multiply returns many times over. Take this simple example: Invest $100 of your own money in a stock that rises to $110 and you make 10 percent. Invest $100 plus $900 of borrowed money in the same stock, for a total of $1,000 invested, and you make $100. You double your money (although you do then have to pay your lender some interest). The problem arises when your investment goes wrong. If the stock drops by 10 percent, then you have wiped out all your own money and still have to pay the interest.

Thus leverage is best left for trades that have a very high probability of making a small amount. In this case, the leverage makes worthwhile an investment that would not otherwise be worth making. Along with chasing trends, the other key job of hedge funds is finding pricing discrepancies and attacking them using leveraged money. This can be a force for making markets more efficient—but if the funds try to keep it going too long, it can create fresh inefficiencies.

As hedge funds evolved, they tended to be small investment vehicles for clubs of wealthy investors run by self-confident managers. Usually, they would have one very specific strategy for making money in particular asset classes—either by attempting to exploit specific inefficiencies and discrepancies in market prices or by following a trend. But then they got bigger.

LTCM had visions of transcending this model. John Meriwether, its founder, had previously been the chief bond trader at Salomon Brothers, giving him a starring role in Michael Lewis's *Liar's Poker*. Apart from other successful traders, bankers, and a former Federal Reserve governor, Meriwether also recruited Myron Scholes and Robert Merton, who had shared a Nobel prize for their part in formulating the Black-Scholes theorem, which made it possible to put a value on options. This team had great credibility and easily raised lots of capital and leverage. Merton was explicit that LTCM was a new kind of "financial intermediary" that would take over roles from banks by borrowing and lending in the capital markets.[2]

Its strategy was to use mathematical models to find securities that were mispriced and then use its money to eliminate the mispricing. When the spread in valuation between two bonds was too wide, according to its models, it would short the expensive one, and buy the cheap one. This way, it could be sure to profit one way or another when the prices moved closer together. At first, it concentrated on technical differences between U.S. government bonds, but as it grew bigger, it needed to look further afield. Roger Lowenstein's classic book *When Genius Failed* details how eventually it held more than half the market for Danish mortgage bonds and had exposures in Brazil, Argentina, Mexico, Venezuela, Korea, Poland, China, Taiwan, Thailand, Malaysia and the Philippines.[3] As with Magellan before it, once it grew big, it had to start treading in areas beyond its traditional remit.

The discrepancies it could identify were often tiny, but with enough leverage they could be profitable. LTCM called this "hoovering up nickels." But few understood just how powerful a vacuum LTCM was using. By its peak in 1998, it had $4.8 billion in its own capital—but it had borrowed so much that it had invested $200 billion. That money came from big banks, who built ever closer and more lucrative relations with hedge funds as regulations eased. Banks profit by holding hedge funds' assets and by lending them money.

LTCM hit problems in the summer of 1998 when Russia defaulted on its debt, as the ripples continued spreading from the previous year's Asia crisis. That default forced losses on many investors and took away their appetite for risk. Risky assets thus tended to fall, relative to safer investments. But LTCM's trades made the opposite bet—that over time different investments would converge. When the world suffered a big enough shock, suddenly all its bets, placed in different markets and countries, became the same thing.

Only small percentage losses would be enough to wipe the fund out because it had so much leverage and it was soon paralyzed. If it failed, it would have to sell $200 billion worth of investments as quickly as possible—and that could have been a disaster. People in the market knew that it was desperate and bet on its investments to keep going down.

Had it fallen, LTCM would have taken others down with it. The market knew that many banks had made big loans to LTCM and stood to lose, or even fail, if the fund failed. No bank felt like lending to another while there was a risk that they stood to suffer such losses, so the corporate credit market dried up. Nobody wanted to trade.

"I've never seen anything like this," admitted Alan Greenspan. "What is occurring is a broad area of uncertainty or fear. When human beings are confronted with uncertainty, meaning they do not understand the rules or the terms of particular types of engagement they're having in the real world, they disengage."[4]

The solution was a meeting at the New York Federal Reserve, where regulators banged together the heads of enough senior bankers to get a deal. All had lent to LTCM and stood to lose. So 14 big banks clubbed together to put $3.5 billion into the fund and in exchange would take it over. The one prominent bank to refuse to join was Bear Stearns.

Did this stoke moral hazard? No taxpayers' funds were used. The LTCM partners themselves were ruined (although most of them bounced back in the next decade). And the money came only from those who had been so foolish as to lend to LTCM in the first place; it was in their self-interest to avert disaster. But Paul Volcker, who usually refrained from criticizing his successor, did not see it that way. He publicly questioned whether it was appropriate for the Fed to "sponsor" a bailout of a private investor that was not a bank.

But if arranging the fund's rescue did not stoke moral hazard, the next act in the drama certainly did. With markets still frozen even after the bailout, Greenspan called an emergency meeting and announced a cut in interest rates an hour before trading closed on a Thursday afternoon. The move, which surprised virtually everyone, ended the crisis and ignited a rally. Bank shares shot up 10 percent within minutes. The incident convinced traders that Greenspan had given up on stamping out "irrational exuberance," and would instead help them if asset prices tumbled.

At least four lessons should have been taken from LTCM. First, even the best mathematical models of markets are prone to break down, so investors should not bet too much borrowed money that they will continue to work. Instead, the models created overconfidence.

Second, any investment strategy devoted to correcting market anomalies has a limited capacity—once enough money has been thrown at correcting a mispricing, the chances are that it will go away. So the more money attempts to follow that strategy, or the longer managers try to make it last, the less successful that strategy will be.

Third, diversification is not what it seems. Given a big enough shock, many apparently different investments can move the same way at once.

And finally, hedge funds cannot work in a vacuum. They have an effect on the environment around them, which affects their capability to take profits.

Thus LTCM should have led to a world of small, highly specialized hedge funds, using little leverage, and returning investors' money to them once their strategy could no longer make profits. Instead, as we will see, almost the opposite happened. And the rate cut that followed to rescue the banks instead prompted investors to dive into the best available opportunity to make a profit. They were about to create the biggest bubble in history—in Internet stocks.

In Summary

- The LTCM rescue was the pivotal event in turning the 1990s bull market into an historic speculative bubble. It led rates lower when they should have been rising and created the belief that governments would always bail out the stock market.

- Hedge funds can use leverage and short-selling to eliminate market inefficiencies, but their fee structure gives them an incentive to exaggerate trends and pile into special situations, making markets more inefficient. By spreading across different markets, they become an extreme force for correlation.

Chapter 13

Dot Coms and Cheap Money

"People still place too much confidence in the markets and have too strong a belief that paying attention to the gyrations in their investments will someday make them rich, and so they do not make conservative preparations for possible bad outcomes."

Robert Shiller in *Irrational Exuberance*

The dot-com boom was the biggest stock market bubble in history—the culmination of decades of cheap money, moral hazard, irrational exuberance, and the herd-like behavior of the investment industry. The response to it prompted the rise of hedge funds and speculative excesses in credit and housing—preconditions for a broader super-bubble.

On November 13, 1998, a few weeks after the LTCM rescue, a start-up company called theglobe.com floated on the NASDAQ stock market. It ran an online community for young New Yorkers with forums such as Harmless Flirts and Soul Mates and a Hot Tub chat room. Everyone wanted to buy. Its shares were offered that morning at $9, and by mid-morning, they were trading for $97 a piece—a rise of 866 percent in two hours.

This insane rush to buy up an obscure Web site that had yet to make a profit showed that the money the Fed had pumped in to the system to revive the banking and credit sectors after LTCM was instead gushing toward the technology sector, which was already over-heated. There was little that could be done to redirect the money. Cutting interest rates stimulates lending across an economy, so it was inevitable that investors would put the money into sectors with growth prospects. Thus low rates to save Wall Street created a bubble in tech stocks.

The NASDAQ boom had other sources of support. The world spent 1999 in the grips of the "Y2K" scare, the fear that computers would stall and shut down when "99" turned to "00" on their internal clocks. The Fed therefore made money available to ensure that such a computer crash did not block bank clients from their money. The bottom lines for the market were cheaper money and more investment in tech stocks. After the millennium turned, without incident, there was one last buying rampage, as NASDAQ stocks moved into a classic investment bubble. Once again, the logic was "safety in numbers." Buy enough Internet start-ups, the logic went, and you would catch a winner or two. They would make you whole for the losses you made as all the others went bust.

There was only so far this argument could go. Google, which proved to be the greatest Internet winner, did not go public until years after the dot-com bubble burst. There was nothing to guarantee that snapping up every new company would yield a long-term winner. But in that environment, almost any start-up could raise funding. Perhaps best remembered is pets.com, an online seller of food and materials for pets, whose omnipresent television advertising featured a dog glove puppet. It went public at $11 per share in February 2000, spent $103 million on sales and marketing—$179 for every customer who ever bought from the site[1]—and then announced an "orderly wind down of its operations" nine months later when its share price had fallen to 9 cents.

Web retailers with little idea how to make money now symbol-ize the era. But even companies with a future were ridiculously overpriced. Cisco Systems, which dominated the market in routers that deliver the Internet to computers, became the biggest company on earth by market value, trading for almost 200 times its most recent earnings. Its share price was $80. Its profits and revenues grew thereafter, yet its share price in early 2010 was $23.

All of this looked as ridiculous at the time as it does now—but nobody had an incentive to blow the whistle on the mania while prices were still going up. When the bubble burst, it did so suddenly and with no obvious cue. On March 10, 2000, a Friday, the NASDAQ reached a peak of 5,132 and suddenly started to fall. After a weekend to think about it, traders sold on the following Monday morning, and from there the fall was swift and almost uninterrupted. When the NASDAQ came to rest more than two years later, it had lost 79 percent of its value.

What happened? Research reports had begun to emphasize companies' "burn rates," or how fast they were burning through their cash. Traders who had previously demanded losses from companies—as this showed that they were investing in new opportunities—finally began to think of their underlying economics. Meanwhile, stock exchange rules barred executives who floated their companies from selling all their shares initially. They were required instead to abstain from selling for a while and watch their fortunes grow on paper. Most companies had only floated a small percentage of their equity when they came to market, and the scarcity helped push up the price. Once the founders started trying to sell, there was in a sense a true market in their shares for the first time. This showed that their true price was much lower.

This was one of history's most absurd investment bubbles and deserves a place beside the seventeenth century Dutch tulip mania. But it was not clear how much impact it would have on the general economy. Many mutual fund investors had only bought in near the top and were left with big losses. And the mania-directed money went into buying advertising for unimaginative Web sites when it could have been invested more productively. But many of the fortunes that were written off had only ever existed on paper. Dot-com millionaires barely had time to spend their wealth before it vanished. The United States went into a recession in 2000, but it was shallow—the briefest since the war. The economies of Western Europe survived without a single quarter of contraction. And the implosion of pets.com and the rest had little impact on other markets—prices of credit, commodities, and foreign exchange were barely affected.

However, Alan Greenspan and the Federal Reserve had their eyes on the economic disasters that had hit after the last two comparable stock market bubbles burst—in the United States in 1929 and in Japan in 1990. Worried that consumers' losses in the stock market would prompt them to spend less and drag the country into deflation, they cut rates. After the September 11 terrorist attacks of 2001, which killed 3,000 and brought down the twin towers of the World Trade Center, and closed down the U.S. stock market for a week, the need to act seemed all the more urgent. The Fed cut its target lending rates to a historic low of 1 percent and left them there.

As with LTCM, after the market got into trouble, the Fed was there to bail them out with lower rates. In the options market, a "put" option gives a buyer the right to sell a stock at a fixed price. It ensures that someone else will have to take the pain for you if the price falls to a certain level. Now, traders talked openly of the "Greenspan Put" and the Fed's credibility—vital in a world no longer anchored to gold—came into question for the first time in two decades. As Figure 13.1 shows, the Fed's behavior in this period certainly made it look as though they would cut interest rates if ever the stock market fell. Traders took note, and stock markets turned around in 2002, when they still looked expensive by historical standards, and then started to rise. Investors' confidence, even after an epic stock market bust, was higher than ever.

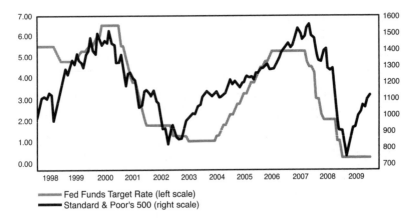

Figure 13.1   *The Greenspan Put? The stock market leads the Fed.*

The victors, ironically, were hedge funds. The NASDAQ crash was a perfect marketing aid for them. Some had actively bet against the bubble by selling short. Others had strategies that did not depend on the stock market and had flourished amid the anxiety from 2000 to 2002. In the first three years of the decade, the S&P 500 lost 9.1 percent, 11.9 percent, and 22.1 percent, respectively. Meanwhile, hedge funds (as measured by Hedge Fund Research, a big Chicago-based research group) gained 4.98 and 4.6 percent before succumbing to a small loss of 1.45 percent in 2002.[2]

Institutions' urge to "chase performance" remained in place. Hedge funds not only appeared to guard against risk; they also made more money than anyone else. Money poured in. Big pension and endowment funds wanted a piece of the action. In 2002, more than $99 billion came into the industry—at the same time that small investors, shaken by the market falls, were pulling $24.7 billion out of mutual funds. Once a phenomenon of the Connecticut suburbs of New York, hedge funds colonized London's Mayfair and established bases in Asia.

The number of funds proliferated. When LTCM went down in 1998, there were 3,325 funds; by 2007 there were more than 10,000. Traders working for banks would set up their own hedge fund to do the same thing for more pay and banks happily accommodated them, giving them room on the trading floor and research for some starting ideas. Generally, new funds planned to invest using strategies that others were already using. They followed similar models, generally based on the theories coming out of academic finance, as synthesized for them by the research departments of big banks, and this led them to the same investments.

In 2005, after four years of persistent inflows, the entire hedge fund industry was worth more than a trillion dollars for the first time. Two years later the industry's assets would peak at more than $1.8 trillion. But this far understated their true power in the market because of their leverage; their true buying power was probably five or six times this much. And they tended to trade furiously, making them far more influential over the day-to-day direction of markets than mutual funds.

The guard had changed again. If the stock market had once been the province of amateurs and then belonged to mutual funds and big institutions, after the NASDAQ crash it was hedge funds that drove prices each day. This was significant because hedge funds, like mutual funds, tend to move in herds. But these herds could move much more widely, as they did not operate under tight remits, and could switch minute by minute between different asset classes and countries. This made them a huge force for interconnectivity between markets. Their use of leverage meant that they might well be forced to sell in haste if their bankers ever got anxious about their ability to repay their loans.

There was another problem. Hedge funds rely on exploiting trends and inefficiencies. With so many funds now leaping into action, inefficiencies disappeared fast. Like mutual funds, they found that size, or at least the number of funds, was the enemy of performance. So they moved quicker, used more leverage, and looked further afield for profits, driving trends as long as they could and throwing money at mispriced securities. Banks were happy to lend to them, generating fees in the process.

None of this helped the entrepreneurs who had briefly been multimillionaires before the NASDAQ bubble burst. By November 2009, shares in theglobe.com, which traded at $97 per share on its debut in 1998, were available for 0.19 cents each. Meanwhile investors needed a new bubble, and they would find it once more in the emerging markets.

In Summary

- The NASDAQ crash of 2000 was a historically extreme event. Rather than allow the U.S. stock market to endure a collapse on the scale seen after earlier bubbles, the Federal Reserve decided to cut rates. This became known as the Greenspan Put.

- Hedge funds made gains during the crash, and this helped them attract new money from investors and rise to dominate the market. Cheaper rates from the Fed helped them boost their returns with leverage.

Chapter 14

BRICs

"Recession-Plagued Nation Demands New Bubble to Invest In"
Headline in www.theonion.com satirical newspaper, July 14, 2008

By rebranding the emerging markets the BRICs (for Brazil, Russia, India, and China), Goldman Sachs ignited a fresh boom. The money pouring into the emerging markets tied them more closely to other stock markets and to commodity markets, as the BRIC stock markets were driven by commodity prices.

"The world needs better economic BRICs," proclaimed Jim O'Neill in November, 2001.[1] Goldman Sachs's chief international economist was making an argument about economic summitry and global politics. He thought the four biggest emerging nations—Brazil, Russia, India, and China—should join major economic decision-making bodies. They were already as big as some of the G7 group of industrialized nations—the United States, Japan, Germany, UK, France, Italy and Canada—whose leaders steered the capitalist world. He showed that they were almost certain to grow bigger. With the world still reeling from the 9/11 terrorist attacks, he was arguing for a sensible realignment in the way global economies were coordinated.

He failed. The BRICs did not take their place at the world's major economic summits until 2009. He succeeded, however, in giving the tired "emerging markets" brand a new lease of life and sparking another gush of money in their direction that also distorted the markets for commodities and foreign exchange.

O'Neill was an economist, not an investment strategist. But the BRICs immediately caught on as an investment strategy. They had a catchy acronym, and eye-catching growth estimates. ("China," O'Neill said, "could overtake Germany by 2007, Japan by 2015, and the United States by 2039. India's economy could be larger than all but the United States and China in 30 years.") The investment industry needed new products after the dot-com bust and the BRICs met that need.

It led to another big idea: "decoupling." Emerging markets largely relied on exporting to the West for their growth. Now, maybe the BRICs would grow by investing in their own infrastructure and catering to the demands of their own growing middle classes. As they built their highways and fed their people, they could "decouple" and grow even if the West was in recession. That promised the holy grail of uncorrelated returns.

Each of the BRICs had plausible stories to tell to investors. More prosaically, after the 1990s crises, emerging markets were dirt cheap. MSCI subsequently started a BRIC index and calculated how it would have performed going back to 1995. In the autumn of 2001, as O'Neill wrote, it was more than 40 percent below where it had been six years earlier.

The BRICs also had luck on their side. Brazil had a presidential election in 2002. Luiz Inácio Lula da Silva, leader in the polls, was a veteran union leader. Money poured out of the country as investors took fright at the prospect of an apparent radical taking over. On the eve of his election, BRICs were down 55 percent from their level of 1995, while Brazil's main stock exchange, the Bovespa, was down 80 percent. Brazilian stocks could be bought for just eight times their earnings—at a time when stocks in the United States traded for

45 times their earnings. When Lula took office, he soon showed himself to be a pragmatist and this spurred an epic emerging market buying opportunity. Anyone who did enough detective work in Brazil could have seen that Lula was not the ogre that many feared and made a killing. But that kind of old-fashioned, on-the-ground detective work was going out of fashion. Instead, "BRIC investing" saw investors herd into index funds as the market took off.

The main driver for these flows of money, whether Western investors realized it or not, was the balance between optimism and pessimism in the West. The logic of decoupling should be straightforward—if emerging markets do well even if times are harsh for the West, then they will be most appealing, relatively, when investors are anxious about the West. But the behavior of MSCI's indexes for the developed world, emerging markets, and the BRICs showed that the opposite was the case. The better the World Index of developed countries did, the more the emerging markets and BRICs outperformed them. If the World did well, BRICs did even better; if the World did badly, BRICs did even worse. Figure 14.1 shows the ironclad relationship that lasted from the beginning of the BRICs boom through to the darkest days of the 2008 crisis. Far from decoupling, emerging markets had coupled to the rest of the world more than ever before. This was a new development—in the 1980s, their performance had been almost totally unrelated, while the 1990s saw a bull market in the West and crisis in the emerging markets (see Figure 14.2).

How did this happen? The BRIC boom was driven by the risk appetites of fund managers and their tendency to move in herds. When investments at home were going well, Western investors had greater tolerance for risk, so funds crowded into the BRICs. When things got worse at home, they got out quick.

Fresh financial innovations helped this. Most emerging markets investing was done through funds that were ultimately linked to an index. And BRICs were ideally suited to the latest new financial products—exchange-traded funds, or ETFs. These are index funds holding a portfolio of shares that aim to match an index but that can be traded on stock exchanges like individual stocks. Their prices change by the minute, and they can be traded swiftly.

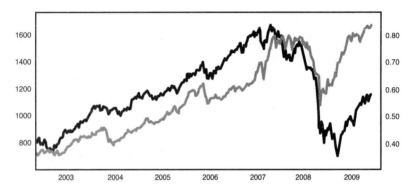

Figure 14.1   *After the BRICs: emerging markets move on sentiment in the West.*

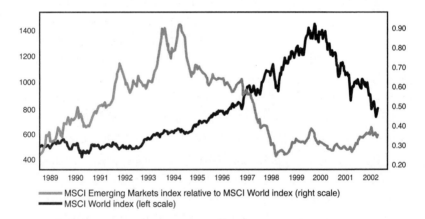

Figure 14.2   *Before the BRICs: emerging markets set their own pace.*

The first ETFs were created early in the 1990s, but they only caught on a decade later. In 2000 and 2001, as stocks crashed, ETFs' assets increased fivefold. From there their growth was rapid, encouraged by stock exchanges that were going public and launching themselves as profit-making concerns, after years of being run as mutual cooperatives.

ETFs are a great idea. They make investing both easier and, for many, cheaper. The problem, as the BRICs boom shows, is the behavior they encourage. Jack Bogle, the inventor of the index fund, contemptuously calls ETFs "a traitor to the cause of classic index investing." "Surely," he argued, "using index funds as trading vehicles can only be described as short-term speculation."[2]

Producing index funds that can trade minute by minute on an exchange could only encourage active trading and attempts to beat the market, he argued—the antithesis of his notion of passive index investing. Like a Purdey shotgun, he said, an ETF "is a great instrument for big game hunting but it is also great for suicide."

ETFs had lower costs than conventional index funds, so they started to track smaller sectors of the stock market or individual countries. While once it had been too difficult to trade minute by minute out of Brazil, for example, and into India—the transaction costs alone involved in transferring the money would make this prohibitively expensive—it was now possible to do so by selling an ETF of Brazilian stocks and buying one devoted to India. This was great for international hedge fund managers surfing on the sums that investors were giving them. Flows became so great that they overwhelmed local factors, so the BRICs traded in line with the West.

Thus it was that in the early years of BRIC investing, hedge funds found that they could use ETFs for the financial equivalent of highly successful big game hunting. Anyone who bought the MSCI's BRIC index at rock bottom, just before Lula was elected, and then held it for five years, would have made a staggering 750 percent. Investing in Brazil alone netted 1600 percent.[3]

As money rolled in, it displaced everything else. There were ways for the market to balance this—an influx should push up the currency, reduce exports, and hence choke off share prices. But it did not work that way. Instead, currencies and stocks, driven by the same investors making the same bet, kept rising. Even Warren Buffett, in 2006, made a big bet on the Brazilian real (which paid off for him).

In the four years from 2005 (a period including the crisis), funds dedicated to the BRIC nations alone grew to have assets of $112 billion and took in $42.2 billion in new money. BRIC-specialist funds accounted for one-third of all funds flowing into emerging markets.

The flows often caused alarm for their recipients. Brazil went in five years from bust to bubble. Daily trading on the Bovespa averaged 2.5 billion reals in 2006. The next year it averaged 4.5 billion reals. And by the end of the year, when the Bovespa itself floated on the market, volume was about 8 billion reals. When it floated, the Bovespa's valuation implied that it was worth about 50 percent more than the London Stock Exchange. Its most obvious weapon to deal with such overheating—raising interest rates—did not help because it attracted even more foreign money from investors buying the currency as part of a carry trade.

These are symptoms of index-led investing—indiscriminate bets on countries and sectors, rather than the on-the-ground detective work that emerging markets investors had once done. But the belief was so strong that the BRICs were a one-way, decoupled bet that they helped to inflate a new "super-bubble" that crossed many asset classes.

The BRICs did deliver in one way. By 2009, O'Neill's forecasts were on track. China's economy overtook Germany's when he said it would. As for their companies, aggregate profits in the BRICs grew at 60 percent per year from 2006 to 2008, until the crash intervened. This was triple the rate of developed countries and double the rate of other emerging countries.[4] International investors helped turn the BRICs into a bubble, but there was real and impressive corporate growth.

The biggest problem with the BRIC idea was that it boiled down to a new way to buy natural resources. If the billions of India and China were at last to receive the living standards of people in the west, they would need to gobble up many commodities to do it. From foodstuffs to industrial metals to oil, the BRIC idea suggested that commodity prices were going up. And that opened up more vistas for financial engineering and synchronized markets.

In Summary

- BRICs investing spurred money into emerging markets. It also pushed up emerging market currencies and commodity prices.
- Thanks to the way the money was invested, with instruments like ETFs, the flows were driven by sentiment in the developed world, not the facts of the emerging world.

Chapter 15

Commodities

We're in a secular bull market in commodities

"We're in a secular bull market in commodities, which started early in 1999.... I went back and looked, and the shortest bull market in commodities I could find lasted 15 years and the longest lasted 23 years. So, if history is any guide, this bull market will last sometime until 2014 and 2022."

Jim Rogers, Commodities Investor

Index investing in commodities opened a new market to mainstream investors and changed the nature of the commodity markets, prompting them to move in line with stocks. It also helped spur huge rises in oil, metals, and food prices and pushed the dollar down.

In 2004, Gary Gorton, a professor at Yale University's School of Management, and Geert Rouwenhoorst from Stanford,[1] published a working paper. Despite its dense mathematics, it became a cult classic for investment managers and sparked institutions to move huge sums into commodities, in the belief that they were not correlated to stocks. In the process, commodities started moving in alignment with stocks.

Their key finding was that commodity futures could be treated as an asset class, like stocks. Over time, commodities were not correlated with equities or bonds, but averaged almost exactly the same return. Different commodities, like heating oil and coffee, had low correlations with each other. Gorton and Rouwenhoorst found that between

104

1959 to 2004, buying and holding a basket of commodity futures delivered average annual returns of 11.5 percent: identical to stocks, only with somewhat lower volatility. This sounds dull, but it meant that a pension fund could reduce its risk by adding commodities to stocks. The expected return was the same, but as commodities were uncorrelated, they would often do well while stocks were doing poorly and vice versa.

One study by Ibbotson Associates for PIMCO went further and found that for any given level of risk, adding commodity futures to a portfolio of stocks, bonds, and cash would increase expected returns. For asset managers required to follow the dictates of modern portfolio theory, which required them to look for uncorrelated assets, these were golden words.[2]

Commodities had long been deep and liquid markets, but they were peopled by producers and their customers. Mainstream investors in stocks and bonds generally steered clear because they lacked detailed knowledge of capacity in each market. Commodity traders knew about piles of copper sitting in warehouses, or the cost of refining oil, or the forecast for the next soybean harvest—factors that did not overlap with stocks and bonds.

The new investors were different. They invested in commodities as an asset class, just as they invested in stocks—passively, through indexes. And so the "financialization" of commodities began: Goldman Sachs and AIG offered indices of futures in different commodities; institutions bought funds linked to them; futures contracts were introduced that were backed by those indices; prices rose; and money piled in.

As with the BRICs, the new interest coincided with a buying opportunity. The oil price bottomed in 1999 at about $12 per barrel. Over the next eight years it rose six-fold, even after inflation was taken into account—equaling the rise from its low in 1973 to the crisis highs in 1980, which inflicted stagflation on the world. From 2007, it doubled again amid the 2008 crisis.

This happened without any of the drastic interruptions to oil supply that hit in the 1970s. And other commodities did even better: Copper rose more than 40 percent in 2005, then rose another 40 percent in 2006. Even soybeans rose more than 80 percent in 2007 alone, sparking food riots across the emerging world. Returns like this attracted a crowd of investors, as commodities became less a superior diversification tool and more about chasing hot performance. Providers of ETFs found a way to let such performance chasers play commodity prices directly. Using futures, banks could underwrite notes that rose or fell in line with commodity prices. These notes would then underpin exchange-traded securities, which proved raucously popular with investors.

Many veteran commodity investors worried both about the influx of new money and about the way it behaved once it hit the market. Commodity futures expire at finite dates. For example, when oil producers want to guarantee a price for April next year, they can sell futures that guarantee the buyer a fixed price the next April. If that buyer is an airline, they now have a handle on their future costs. Speculators' normal role is to act as go-betweens between producers and suppliers and make money on short-term rises and falls while doing so. The notion of index investors passively buying and holding commodities was a new one for the market. As each futures contract neared its expiration, index funds would sell it and buy into the future for the next month, often making a profit in the process. Behaving this way arguably put upward pressure on prices.

This generated controversy, and in 2008 the U.S. Senate held hearings on the issue. Senator Joseph Lieberman called for limits on index investing. "We may need to limit the opportunity people have to maximize their profits because a lot of the rest of us are paying through the nose, including some who can't afford it," he said.[3]

These arguments rest on the circumstantial evidence that commodity prices rose as money poured into index funds. Detailed academic studies have so far failed to find a causal link between the two. But the influx of new money may well have affected commodities' low correlation with other assets. Gary Gorton, whose paper on commodities' low correlations helped fire institutions' interest, stands by those findings for the long term. "You can argue whatever you want about the last three years, two years, one year, six months. That's not how we do research," he told the *Financial Times* in 2010. But he concedes the possibility that the influx of money had an effect. "There were people who traded in equities and people who traded in commodities and they were different groups. To the extent that they became the same group, there's a tendency for those correlations to become positive," he said.[4] He pointed to the experience of Mexican companies when they take out a dual listing in the United States to attract U.S. investors—and generally start to correlate more with U.S. markets.

There is another problem, which echoes the objections to the research that attracted Michael Milken to high-yield bonds. Commodities were indeed uncorrelated assets when they were not treated as their own asset class, but there was an issue of capacity. While low-grade bonds or commodities remained areas for specialists who did not touch other markets, they might well outperform other markets and stay uncorrelated with them. Once more money entered and investors with different motivations and behaviors started relying on the old relationships to hold, there was reason to fear that they would not stay uncorrelated.

As the oil price rose, traders found other ways to rationalize the spike. They clung to the theory of "Peak Oil"—the idea that the world's production of oil has peaked and started a gradual decline. At some point, of course, this theory will come true. Supply rose somewhat in the early years of the oil rally, so Peak Oil does not explain the entire rally. But in 2007, supply slipped, fueling Peak Oil theorists.

These arguments needed geologists to resolve them, rather than economists, but as oil rose, so the classic bubble psychology took over and many believed falling supply caused the price rises.

Another rationalization came from a much older theory. Nikolai Kondratieff, a Marxist revolutionary executed by Stalin in the 1930s, left behind a theory that commodity prices follow "super-cycles," each lasting a decade or two. Periods of stagnant commodity prices would be followed by decade-long periods when they rose. This had implications for stocks. Stocks had stagnated when Kondratieff "waves" were pushing commodity prices upward, as in the 1970s and the 1930s. When commodities were stable, as in the 1980s and 1990s, stocks gained.[5] So investors latched on to the notion of a "super-cycle" and protected themselves against problems for equities by stockpiling oil and metals.

But commodities' relationship with stocks did not work the way it was supposed to. History had shown a long-term *negative* correlation between oil and share prices. In other words, as the oil price goes up, companies' costs increase and their profits fall, so their share prices should go down. But now, high commodity prices turned into an argument for buying stocks. In particular, the oil and metals markets had a mutually reinforcing relationship with China. In 2006, the extra or marginal Chinese demand for oil accounted for 72 percent of the total growth in oil consumption across the world.[6] Such extreme pressure from demand justified rising prices.

With resources companies making up 69 percent of the market value of the BRIC countries (compared to 39 percent globally),[7] BRICs and commodities reinforced each other. If Chinese stocks were rising, this was a sign of increasing demand for commodities, so investors should buy them. If commodities were rising, then China was hungry for growth, so buy China. Shanghai's stock market doubled in 2006 and entered a bubble in 2007. That was taken as a reason to buy oil and metals—even though higher oil prices should be a problem for a big importer like China.

The argument was different for other emerging markets. Russia's economy is almost wholly dependent on oil. Latin America is rich in metals. But as Figure 15.1 shows, the price of MSCI's Latin American index, which is dominated by Brazil, came to correlate perfectly with moves in the prices of industrial metals. In effect, Brazil was being priced as though it were one large copper mine—but in fact, it is a more diversified economy than that (and a surprisingly closed one). With exports making up only 14 percent of its GDP, this correlation was plainly taken too far.

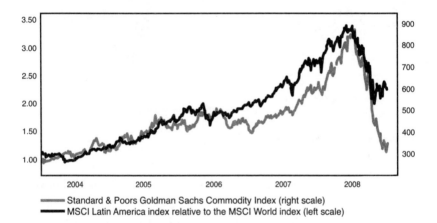

Standard & Poors Goldman Sachs Commodity Index (right scale)
MSCI Latin America index relative to the MSCI World index (left scale)

Figure 15.1 *Commodity prices drive Latin American stocks.*

Rising commodity prices also had an impact on currencies. If copper prices rise in dollars, then Brazilian copper miners receive more dollars for every ounce of copper they sell. This flow of money pushes up the Brazilian currency. More significantly, almost all commodity transactions are denominated in dollars. If a dollar is worth less, then commodity prices must rise to reflect this. So worries that the dollar would fall translated into rising commodity prices, rising commodity prices translated into a lower dollar, and traders knowing about this relationship could hedge against a weaker dollar by buying commodities. The correlation between the dollar and the oil price grew absurdly tight (see Figure 15.2).

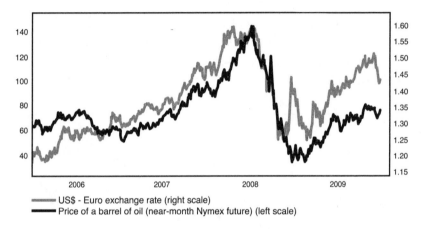

US$ - Euro exchange rate (right scale)
Price of a barrel of oil (near-month Nymex future) (left scale)

Figure 15.2 *The dollar and oil: in lock-step*

Carry traders, of course, took even greater advantage by borrowing cheaply in yen. Currencies backed by resource-rich countries, such as Australia, New Zealand, and South Africa, rose dramatically. The carry trade money could then be recycled into BRIC stocks or into commodities.

The sum effect of all this activity was to push up commodity prices ever further, taking emerging currencies with them. The forces driving currencies, commodities, and emerging markets became indistinguishable and all were ultimately driven by the appetite for risk of traders in the western stock markets. None of this is normal. Commodities, like exchange rates, are supposed to be balancing mechanisms. If demand exceeds supply, prices rise until demand drops again—continued rising prices choke off the economy, as they did in the 1970s. But financializing commodities turned this logic on its head and drove a self-reinforcing synchronized bubble. All it needed to inflate it to a scale that could endanger the entire global economy was an injection of artificially cheap credit—and financial engineers could provide it.

In Summary

- Index investing in commodities as an asset class contributed to a big bull market that also pushed up emerging markets' stocks and currencies.
- Historical relationships between commodities and stocks were reversed and commodities moved more closely in line with equities.

Chapter 16

Credit

"Directors noted that the rapid growth in recent years of credit derivative and structured credit markets had facilitated the dispersion of credit risk by banks to a broader, more diverse group of investors, making the financial system more resilient and stable. However, directors observed that these markets had grown rapidly in a relatively benign environment and had not been fully tested."

IMF Global Financial Stability Report, 2006

The credit market boom of the mid-2000s, especially in subprime mortgages, sparked a scandal of historic proportions. Derivatives enabled investors to spread credit risk and gave the impression that the risk of default throughout the economy had reduced. In fact, they made funding artificially cheap for speculative investments worldwide.

In September 2005, the New York Federal Reserve summoned 14 international bankers to its headquarters for their first meeting since the LTCM crisis seven years earlier. This time, conditions were calm, but the Fed saw risks on the horizon. The bankers were the leading dealers of new instruments known as credit default swaps and the message to them was blunt: "Clean up your act or we will do it for you."

The Fed's alarm, we now know, was prescient. It wanted to take action because credit derivatives had grown faster than the banks could process them. Even the paperwork was a mess. More than any other innovation, they fostered the belief that investors now knew how to tame risk. But as with any new technology, they carried risks of their own.[1] Further, they stripped banks of their most important role, assessing the risk of default, and turned it over to the markets. Sure enough, soon after the Fed's meeting the synchronized bubble entered its most destructive stage, fueled in large part by credit.

In concept, credit default swaps are simple. Take this example. A bank has a relationship with General Motors, which wants an extra $1 billion loan. The bank wants to maintain its relationship, but feels uncomfortable about being so exposed to one company. A rival bank has had a similar request from Ford, and has the same dilemma.

The solution is for the banks to "swap" half of their exposure so that each is on the hook for loans of $500 million to each company. Now if one of the car companies gets into trouble, the banks will bear the exposure to it equally. Both maintain their relationships but have a more prudent spread of risks. The car companies benefit because the banks are stronger and more able to offer financing in the future.

Such a transaction is simpler to describe than to execute, as the legal structures are very complicated. But once lawyers and financiers hit on a workable template, the idea took off and swiftly developed. Rather than swapping exposure to two different lenders, investors could swap corporate exposure for exposure to the U.S. government, which was deemed almost riskless. In such a transaction, the holder of the loan buys their way out of that risk, while a large bank or insurer assumes it. In effect, it is an easily obtained form of insurance.

The price of the transaction thus shows the risk that the loan will default. If $1 of General Motors risk is swapped for 95 cents of Treasury bond risk for a period of five years, then that puts the risk of a GM default within the next five years at 5 percent. As the deals were standardized, they were collated, and dealers could track default risk on their screens minute by minute.

As in any market, default risk prices grew prone to overshooting in either direction. While greed was in the ascendant, it was very easy to insure against default—and cheap insurance encouraged investors to buy too much debt. If fear took the upper hand, the supply of debt could dry up suddenly.

Default risks could be swapped more than once. As big banks busily swapped the same risks time and again, they created mind-boggling figures. In 2001, the first year anyone tried to measure the burgeoning phenomenon, the total amount of debt that had been "swapped" came to about $650 billion, according to the International Swaps and Derivatives Association. In the second half of 2007, it peaked at $62 *trillion*—greater than the gross domestic product of the world at the time.[2]

As with the booms in BRICs and commodities, the innovation came when it was possible to buy cheap. Low interest rates in the United States—imposed in the wake of the dot-com bust—made credit transactions possible that would not have made sense at higher rates.

And rates stayed low. Greenspan and the Federal Reserve raised rates repeatedly, with their target rate reaching 5.25 percent in the summer of 2006. But the Fed can only directly move short-term rates. The more important rate for the credit markets that financed longer-term transactions was the yield paid on ten-year treasury bonds. This set their implicit "risk-free" rate. If treasury yields went up, then the yields on riskier credit would have to rise too, even if the risk of default was unchanged.

But bond yields refused to rise, enabling the credit boom to carry on for years. Alan Greenspan called this a "conundrum." The most likely answer lies in the demand for bonds. China, with other Asian countries, was building foreign reserves, buying dollars and parking them in U.S. treasury bonds. In 2000, China had $157 billion in foreign reserves; by 2009 it had more than $2 trillion—a huge weight of money pushing treasury yields down.

With baseline interest rates low, the ability to isolate and trade default risk lent itself to new transactions. Without lending to a company, bankers could create a "synthetic" investment that mimicked such a loan, its value rising and falling with the risk of default. This levered the system all the more. If a company defaulted, the total cost to investors might be higher than the amount of debt that had defaulted, because many had deliberately chosen to take on a risk that mimicked that default.

By the middle of the decade, when the Fed called in the bankers, greed was ascendant. Market prices implied not only that risks had been shared, but also that default risk across the entire economy had been reduced. A mathematical way to do this is to look at the yields paid on corporate bonds compared to treasury bonds and then work out what level of defaults would be needed to bring the total amount they pay to investors down to the same level.

Jim Reid, an analyst at Deutsche Bank in London, calculated that by 2007, "single-B" junk bonds were so expensive that they could only make money compared to Treasuries if they went on to have a lower default over the following five years than had been seen at any time over the previous three decades. As many at that time feared a recession, which would raise defaults, these prices made no sense.

Further, the technology for corporate credit was soon also applied to mortgages. By providing cheap insurance, it made it possible to invest in mortgages for subprime borrowers with poor credit histories. Such people are bad credit risks by definition, but diversification could help. Lend to enough subprime borrowers and a lot will repay—and if you can insure easily through the market, the lowered risk might be worth taking. Then factor in the housing market—even if the borrower defaults, lenders get to repossess the house, and house prices were rising. Then came another layer of alchemy: bundling many different mortgages into packages known as collateralized debt obligations (CDOs) and then slicing each bundle into so-called "tranches." For example, investors might buy a tranche representing 10 percent of the mortgage pool, which would bear the first losses. So if the default rate for the entire pool were as high as 10 percent, this tranche would be wiped out. These tranches offer risky investments.

But a tranche representing the last 50 percent of the mortgage pool to default looked very safe. Providing only that the default rate for the whole pool did not exceed 50 percent, a huge number even for subprime mortgages, its investors would be repaid in full. Such "super-senior" debt could get triple-A ratings, allowing banks to hold on to it under their newly permissive regulations at no cost. They could sell the riskier tranches, hold on to the safer ones, and use the money they had generated to go out and buy more loans. As with junk bonds and emerging markets before them, there was "safety in numbers."

And investors believed that they were truly safe. Market prices allowed a clear measure of default risk, which could be measured with the ABX index, introduced by Markit, where 100 implied a zero default rate, and 0 implied a total default. In early 2007, on the eve of financial catastrophe, the ABX index of subprime mortgages stood above 95, implying that less than 5 percent of subprime mortgages would default.

With hindsight, this episode can already be seen as one of the greatest scandals in U.S. history. Many lenders and borrowers behaved disgracefully, and regulators should never have allowed them to do so. But it was financial innovation that enabled them. The agents who made loans had been separated from the principals who bore the risk of those loans, and banks' decline gave them an incentive to behave badly. The sum effect was to give debtors—whether smaller companies or subprime homeowners—credit at prices far cheaper than ever before.

That cheap credit fed into other markets and inflated them. House prices shot up in the United States and in countries like the UK and Spain. While house prices—lenders' collateral—were rising, subprime lending seemed easy to justify, so more lending led to still higher prices. The cheap credit also drove the stock market.

Companies can finance themselves by either debt or equity. Usually equity, in which their investors are entitled to a share of earnings, is cheaper for them. In other words, usually earnings as a proportion of the price of the shares they issue are lower than interest payments as a proportion of the debt they issue.

But now, debt was cheaper for companies than equity, so corporate managers could boost their market value by borrowing money to buy up their own shares. This reduced the supply of shares in circulation and thus pushed up the value of each remaining share for shareholders. By the spring of 2007, U.S. companies were spending $3 billion each day doing this, according to the research group TrimTabs. Activist investors poured their energy into forcing companies to take on more debt or to pay out big dividends.

Money also poured into private equity funds, the new name for what in Michael Milken's era had been called corporate raiders. Nine of the ten biggest leveraged buy-outs in U.S. history happened in 2006. In Europe, where stocks had traditionally traded at lower multiples to earnings, equity finance was more expensive for companies, and this financial engineering made even more sense.

Thus credit and stock markets grew interlinked. Stock market growth rested on cheap credit, not any underlying growth, and Western companies were under pressure to borrow rather than to invest in growth opportunities. Again, it was unclear which markets were driving up which others—they had become a mutually reinforcing cycle.

It is easy to see, therefore, why the Fed tried to scare the big banks behind all this activity. Fatefully, however, the bankers got their act together just enough to satisfy their supervisors. "These institutions have taken this thing seriously, as have their regulators," said Gerald Corrigan, the former New York Fed governor charged with breathing down the banks' necks, in late 2006. "So far so good in terms of damage control."[3] But Corrigan carefully did not declare victory, which was just as well. A few months later, the extent of the interconnections between markets, and of the overconfidence they had fueled, would be made brutally obvious. The correlated and fearful rise of markets was ready to turn into a synchronized sell-off.

In Summary

- Credit default swaps started as a risk-management tool but enabled the systemic underpricing of credit. This made financing cheaper and pushed up prices of assets across the world.
- Critically, credit derivatives enabled funds to flow toward subprime mortgage borrowers. This blew up the synchronized bubble to unsustainable proportions.

Part II

The Fall

Chapter 17

Ending the Great Moderation

> *"Stability—even of an expansion—is destabilizing in that more adventuresome financing of investment pays off to the leaders and others follow. Thus an expansion will, at an accelerating rate, feed into the boom."*
>
> Hyman P. Minsky, writing in 1975

Bubbles require low volatility and low interest rates, which make financial engineering possible. When volatility rose with the February 2007 "Shanghai Surprise," followed by a rise in long-term interest rates, the super-bubble was ready to burst.

February 27, 2007 dawned, like all other days, in the East. It was a slow news day in Asia, but for some reason Shanghai traders started selling. Even after the mandatory midday break in trading, they kept selling. By the close, the Shanghai Composite, index for the biggest stock market in China—where many of the world's hopes now resided—was down 9 percent for its worst day in a decade.

Traders in London and Frankfurt seemed mesmerized. European stock market fell, wiping out their gains for the year. Falls at the opening in Wall Street were a *fait accompli* after such awful overnight news. But the worst of the day was yet to come. Sell orders built up and became ever harder to process in the afternoon thanks to the market's official "circuit-breaker" mechanisms that blocked traders from making big sales of stock unless share prices were ticking up. These rules had been in place since the 1997 Hong Kong crash forced New York's stock exchange to close early, but they did not help. Instead, big "sell" orders banked up until suddenly the exchange's computers caught up.

At 2:57 that afternoon, the Dow Jones Industrial Average stood at 12,346.33—down about 2 percent for the day. By 3:02, as computers finally caught up, it had dropped to 12,089.02—off more than 540 points for the worst day since the 9/11 terrorist attacks some five years earlier. Those few minutes shook the confidence of traders around the world. This day, destined to be known as the "Shanghai Surprise," ended the years of the "Great Moderation."[1]

The "Great Moderation," a phrase used by economists, refers to the way the world economy grew with low volatility after the Federal Reserve under Paul Volcker tamed inflation in the early 1980s. Recessions were shorter and shallower. But during the Great Moderation in the economy, markets were as volatile as ever—which is not surprising, as markets' daily movements reflect mass psychology more than the economy. Then, as the credit boom took hold, they enjoyed a moderation of their own.

Volatility or fear can be measured using options prices. The Chicago Board Options Exchange's Vix Index tracks the cost of insuring against future volatility in the stock market. The more investors are prepared to spend on options to protect against future volatility, the higher the Vix, which is nicknamed the "fear gauge." The Vix peaked above 45 during the LTCM crisis. Normally, volatility itself is volatile, with brief spasms punctuating longer periods when markets are stable.

This was not the story of the middle years of the first decade of the twenty-first century. As Figure 17.1 shows, volatility dropped to historic lows and stayed there, due to artificially cheap credit. While credit is too cheap, markets can stay calm and in early 2007, the Vix dipped below 10 for the first time ever. On the Shanghai Surprise day, it rose by almost 60 percent to reach 18 and never retreated, ending the Great Moderation in the markets.

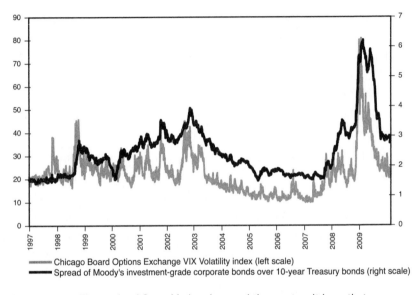

Chicago Board Options Exchange VIX Volatility index (left scale)
Spread of Moody's investment-grade corporate bonds over 10-year Treasury bonds (right scale)

Figure 17.1 *The markets' Great Moderation—and the great meltdown that followed*

Viewed in this context, we can see that the Surprise was less unusual than the moderation that preceded it. Arguably the reaction that day, and the violent volatility that followed, were even caused by the markets' Great Moderation. This is exactly what Hyman Minsky, a maverick and largely overlooked left-wing economist, would have argued. The Surprise came just as many were looking at his work anew. Minsky argued that periods of moderation allowed some lenders to offer excessive credit, which forced other players to offer credit too cheaply until the cumulative excesses caused a speculative collapse. Without healthy regular doses of fear, he thought markets and banks would do something stupid. Low volatility made it easier and safer to take on debt, which would in turn smooth out volatility. As the perceived risk of corporate default fell, as shown in Figure 17.1, by the extra yield on corporate bonds compared to government bonds, so stock market volatility fell in almost perfect alignment.

The artificial stability of mid-decade, he would have suggested, unleashed a desperate race to extend credit on more generous terms. As he put it: "As a boom develops, households, firms, and financial institutions are forced to undertake ever more adventuresome position-making activity. When the limit of their ability to borrow from one to repay another is reached, the option is to either sell out some position or to bring to a halt, or slow down, asset acquisition."[2]

This describes what transpired in 2007. The causes of the Shanghai Surprise are unimportant compared to the fact that it happened. Volatility for its own sake wrought a huge change in what financial engineers could do. It turned the carry trade into a risky proposition, and so as risk increased, investors rushed to buy the yen. Hence the yen and the U.S. stock market, after decades of being unrelated, suddenly became tightly correlated on the day of the Surprise. Both were responding minute by minute to changes in the market's appetite for risk.

Volatility made transactions based on short-term credit—by this point a huge chunk of the market—inherently more risky. So much borrowed money lay behind the positions that had been built up that markets could turn violently as soon as it fled. Traders looked at the assumptions undergirding the markets' Great Moderation, asked if they believed them, and decided that they didn't.

This, rather than anything that happened in Shanghai, explains what happened. The incident was not about contagion from China. Instead, a different dynamic was at work: correlation. "The global macro backdrop to all of this is that almost every asset is more highly correlated to every other," one trader confided to the *Financial Times* that day. "Chinese consumers and Joe Public in Detroit are no longer as dissimilar as they used to be."[3]

The risks emanating from the United States were clear and menacing. More than 20 subprime lenders had filed for bankruptcy, and the ABX Index, measuring the cost of insuring against default, made the fear transparent for all. In January, it implied that there would be no defaults on that year's mortgages. By the Shanghai Surprise two months later, it was predicting a default rate of almost 40 percent. That had alarming implications for U.S. consumers and hence the Chinese exporters who sell to them.

Therefore, many different investors in different markets made the same judgment on the same day to get out of the market. China happened to come first. Markets were so interconnected that it took traders in Shanghai to alert U.S. traders to problems in the American credit market

In the weeks after this shock, markets recovered, although volatility remained higher. There was even a final splurge of mortgage issuance. Thanks to herd psychology, many bankers made the same calculation: While others were taking risks, and profiting, there was nothing to do but join them. Bankers, like mutual fund managers, were judged against their peers. Chuck Prince, then the CEO of Citigroup, explained this with an unforgettable metaphor that became his epitaph when he was forced to resign months later. "When the music stops, in terms of liquidity, things will be complicated," he confided to the *Financial Times*. "But as long as the music is playing, you've got to get up and dance. We're still dancing."[4]

It took the bond market to bring that dance to an end and also end the economic Great Moderation itself. Bond traders rely heavily on the patterns they can discern in trading charts. And long-dated treasury bonds, the "risk-free" securities that provide a baseline for pricing assets throughout the financial world, were in the grips of a strong and reliable long-term trend.

Bond yields follow a cycle, rising when central banks are tightening interest rates. But since Volcker had tamed inflation, each successive peak had been lower than the one that preceded it. A perfectly straight downward-sloping line joined the peaks. Inflation will eat away at the value of payments made by long-dated bonds, meaning that rising expectations for inflation will push down bond prices, while pushing up yields. Thus this downward trend showed faith that inflation was steadily being squeezed out of the system—a symptom of the economic Great Moderation.

But after the Shanghai Surprise, bond yields rose menacingly. So much easy credit would only be expected to fan the flames of inflation. Traders asked whether the longstanding assumption of permanently falling inflation could stand. They decided it could not.

On June 7, 10-year yields reached 5.05 percent. As Figure 17.2 shows, this apparently unremarkable event breached the downward trend line for the first time in 22 years. Traders all around the world instantly recognized the significance and panic ensued. Everyone wanted to dump bonds. Yields shot up. And with this, the second vital support for the imaginative financial engineering of the markets' Great Moderation had been kicked away.

This had a direct effect on credit investments, which are priced with respect to treasury bond yields—the higher the risk, the higher the extra "spread" compared to treasuries the borrower will have to pay. When bond yields rose, traders had no choice. They could not reduce still further their estimate of the extra risk their investments carried compared to Treasuries. Fresh subprime bankruptcies made that impossible.

So they had to accept that the extra spreads they were paying were far too low and would need to increase to reflect the true risk. That meant raising the interest rates paid out on higher risk bonds to a point where they were no longer affordable for borrowers, along with cutting the price of debt for anyone wanting to sell it in the secondary market. The scene was set for the prices of structured credit investments to go into free-fall.

10-year Treasury bond yield

Figure 17.2 *A breach in the trend: bond yields spiked up in the summer of 2007*

In Summary

- The financial engineering behind the bubble relied on low volatility and low rates. Hyman Minsky showed these can drive higher volatility. Once they had been removed, the structures could not stand.

- It was the treasury bond market that called time on the bubble—and it may well play that role again in the future.

Chapter 18

Quant Funds

"Because of the lack of transparency and coordination within the hedge-fund industry and the strong relationship between performance and business viability, competitive pressures will lead managers and prime brokers to increase leverage in an 'arms race' for generating better returns."
Andrew W. Lo of Massachusetts Institute of Technology

Too much money tends to chase good ideas until they get overcrowded, setting up a crash when the crowd goes the other way. When the same investors crowd into many different investments, as quant funds did in 2007, the herd can move in surprising directions. This happened when a credit hedge fund asked its lenders for leniency in June 2007 and sparked a crisis for unrelated quantitative equity funds.

On June 19, 2007, a few days after the bond market revolt, a hedge fund run by Bear Stearns, Wall Street's fifth biggest broker, asked its creditors for a rescue.[1] The High-Grade Structured Credit Strategies Enhanced Leverage fund had raised about $600 million from investors and then borrowed another $6 billion against it. That leverage would have multiplied investors' returns many times over if the fund's investments rose in value. Unfortunately, the fund was invested in securities backed by subprime mortgages, and it was obvious that their value was falling.

The fall-out when Bear tried to get out of the mess was a moment of truth for the credit market. It also savagely demonstrated that markets were interconnected by inflicting sweeping losses on investments that had nothing to do with mortgages.

The leverage came from other large Wall Street banks, and Bear wanted them to forego interest payments for a year to relieve the pressure on the fund. This was a lot to ask, and the request was refused. Instead, the banks demanded the securities, mostly packages of subprime debt that had been stuck together and resold known as CDOs, that Bear had pledged to them as collateral for the loans. At their purchase price, the CDOs covered the value of the loans.

But CDOs were not designed to be traded. The idea was to buy and then hold them until all the loans within them had been repaid, and there was barely any secondary market for them. If the creditors wanted their money back, they would have to sell the CDOs in the market. This they tried to do by holding auctions. And so it was that a raft of subprime securities suddenly hit the market on June 20. This revealed a basic truth—nobody was quite sure what the securities were worth, so nobody wanted to buy them. As with dot-com stocks seven years earlier, CDOs had stayed overpriced on paper only because nobody tried to sell them on the market, at least in any volume.

This was credit markets' "Wile E. Coyote" moment. The character in the old Warner Brothers Roadrunner cartoons would run off the edge of a cliff and keep running in defiance of gravity. Then he would stop and look down. Then, and only then, he would fall, a look of exasperated resignation on his face. In much the same way, markets ran off a cliff on the Shanghai Surprise. The need to maintain the fiction that their subprime investments were worth something kept them running. Rising bond yields made the fiction harder to sustain by forcing up rates and making it harder for borrowers to repay their loans. When the Bear CDOs finally hit the market, the coyote had no choice but to look down. And he could no longer defy gravity.

That meant trouble for banks with similar CDOs on their balance sheet. Cold evidence from the market suggested they were overpriced, but marking down their price meant cutting the very value of the banks' assets. Given how much banks had borrowed against those CDOs, it might have meant admitting that they were insolvent—which explains why the fictionally high values were maintained for so long.

Bear, the funds' parent, bailed out a similar, less leveraged fund at a cost of a $1.6 billion, plus a lasting blow to the bank's credibility. It eventually had to admit that the Enhanced Leverage fund had lost all its value.[2] With this, faith in subprime securities was irreparably damaged—and that loss of faith rippled through interconnected world markets to inflict losses in an unlikely place.

The next victims were a group of computer-driven hedge funds whose investments had virtually nothing to do with subprime mortgages. "Market-neutral" or "long/short" hedge funds practice an arcane form of investing. They borrow and then sell stocks in companies that seem overvalued (setting up a profit if their price falls) and balance those bets by putting the money into stocks that they believe to be undervalued.

This is called "market-neutral" because the direction of the market should not matter. If it goes down, the "short" positions will make money, and the "long" positions will lose. If the market rises, it will be the other way around. All that matters is that the managers select their stocks right, and spot which are relatively over- and under-priced. To avoid betting that some sectors will do better than others, many funds pair stocks in the same industry, so a bet against General Motors might be balanced by a bet in favor of Ford.

The subprime mess was bad news for the market as a whole because it implied that consumers would have less money to spend. But falling prices for mortgage-backed bonds should not affect a bet that Ford would outperform General Motors. Such news might cause the price of both stocks to fall, but that would mean making money on the short position in GM to balance the loss on Ford stock. In any case, the funds invested only in publicly traded stocks, not the kind of illiquid, infrequently traded securities that can lead to mispricing and accidents.

But between August 7 and August 9, some of the most famous names on Wall Street took terrible losses investing this way. The Global Equity Opportunities Fund, flagship of Goldman Sachs, lost slightly more than 30 percent of its value that week. Goldman had to join Bear Stearns in putting up money—$2 billion in this case—to help out one of its hedge funds. They were not alone. Many others suffered similar fates in a week when the stock market as a whole was relatively quiet.

These funds turned out to be exposed to mortgages. Piecing together what happened is difficult, but detective work by Andrew Lo, a hedge fund expert at the Massachusetts Institute of Technology, looked convincing—and convinced many of the hedge fund managers themselves who took losses that week.[3] On August 6, he believed, one big long-short fund liquidated its positions, buying back the stocks it had shorted and selling the stocks it held.

Why would it have done this? Many hedge funds are ultimately owned by funds of hedge funds, a popular way for investors to get a stake in the market. A fund of funds that had just suffered a loss on its credit investments or could not get money out of a credit fund might well decide instead to ask for their money back from a long-short fund.

Or the fund that started liquidating may have faced a demand from its lenders. That could have been critical. Long-short strategies do not appear risky, but they also do not make much money—unless borrowed money is thrown in. Returns of 1 or 2 percent per year get much more interesting if they are multiplied ten times by leverage. Lenders alarmed by credit losses needed to call in loans where they could, which might mean demanding money back from a long-short fund.

When Professor Lo attempted to map how market-neutral funds would have done that week, he found they would have lost 6.8 percent in three days—far worse than anything before experienced. That they in fact lost as much as 30 percent can be attributed to leverage. Once that leverage was removed, the bubble that it had inflated had to pop. By getting out, the first fund caused its "short" positions to rise, and its "long" positions to fall. That created losses for the many other funds that, guided by the same models, had made the same bets. The losses made it harder for them to meet the demands from their creditors, so they also exited, inflicting even worse losses on those who were still holding on to those positions. The funds had backed their bets with so much borrowed money that they now drove certain stocks' prices. In the market vernacular, these were "crowded trades."

How had this happened? In 2000 or 2001, when hedge funds had less money to play with, they could make such bets and make money even as the market was tumbling. But that had attracted far more money into the funds, and there were no longer enough mispriced shares to go around. With so much money doing the same thing, those mispricings tended to be corrected quickly and profits were harder to come by.

This created exactly the dilemma that faced Fidelity's Magellan fund a decade earlier. They could have responded by closing shop and returning money to investors. But they had an alternative that was not open to a regulated mutual fund, which was to borrow up to the hilt and improve returns that way. This meant pumping unnaturally large sums of money into the same bets. Leverage, a force for keeping the market efficient a few years earlier, now became a vehicle for distorting value through booms and busts.

Many of the investors themselves believed that the crash that befell them was literally impossible. David Viniar, the chief financial officer of Goldman Sachs, went so far as to tell the *Financial Times* that the market had suffered events so implausible that they were "25 standard deviation moves, several days in a row."[4]

In a bell curve, events deviate only from the norm by as much as three standard deviations 1 percent of the time. A 25 standard deviation event is so unusual that it might never happen in the history of the universe. So by saying this, Mr. Viniar was either saying that these events had not in fact happened—or that the statistical models that had produced the estimated standard deviations in the first place were faulty.

While flawed, none of this was illegal. Prosecutors tried to convict the Bear Stearns funds' managers of fraud and failed. They were found not guilty by a jury in Manhattan in November, 2009.[5] Quant funds survived and suffered less than other investors during the disasters of 2008. But the damage had been done. And now, mortgages were about to infect the money market itself.

In Summary

- When creditors of a troubled Bear Stearns hedge fund auctioned its mortgage-backed securities, it became clear that nobody knew what they were worth. That led to withdrawal of cheap leverage from the whole system.

- Cheap leverage allows hedge funds to boost returns from strategies that are minimally profitable and should otherwise be abandoned. Instead, their trades get "overcrowded," leading to crashes when leverage leaves.

- Quantitative models brought many investors into the same investments, but they did not model the effects that such crowding would have.

Chapter 19

Trust

"No, sir, the first thing is character. Before money or anything else. Money cannot buy it. Because a man I do not trust could not get money from me on all the bonds in Christendom."

J.P. Morgan, when asked in 1913 if money or property was the basis of commercial credit

Financial markets rely on trust. Uncertainty over the location of subprime losses caused a crisis of confidence in the summer of 2007. Central bank intervention averted disaster, as markets still trusted governments and central banks. But this intensified the problem of moral hazard.

"The Fed is asleep!" yelled Jim Cramer, CNBC's pundit-in-chief. "We have Armageddon. In the fixed-income markets, we have Armageddon." On August 3, 2007, he descended into a five-minute tirade against the Fed, where the former Princeton University economist Ben Bernanke had replaced Alan Greenspan a year earlier. "Bernanke is being an academic! It is no time to be an academic. He has no idea how bad it is out there. He has no idea! He has no idea!" he screamed on live television. "My people have been in this game for 25 years. And they are losing their jobs and these firms are going to go out of business, and he's nuts! They're nuts! They know nothing!"[1]

As trading room television sets tend to be switched to CNBC, in large part to see Cramer, the rant had an impact. Even though money markets had usurped the roles once played by banks, they were left unheeded most of the time, and it was news to most investors that they were in trouble. Cramer now revealed that the problem for mortgages had infected the price of money itself.

He also waded into the debate over moral hazard. The "Greenspan Put," with lower interest rates whenever the market got into trouble, had helped markets rise to this point. Some at the Fed wanted to take a stand and force markets to realize that there was no "put" if the market went down. "The punishment has been meted out to those who have done misdeeds and made bad judgments," said Bill Poole, governor of the St. Louis Fed. "We are getting good evidence that the companies and hedge funds that are being hit are the ones who deserve it."

Cramer argued that distaste for moral hazard was for "academics" like Poole, whom he called "shameful." The theories looked good on paper, but in the real world they did not make sense. Too many people could be hurt by a central bank attempt to show them that there were real risks out there.

The problem boiled down to a loss of trust that worked its way out in a few dozen dealing rooms across the world and was virtually invisible to anyone on the outside. An analogy from Harry Potter illustrates the problem.[2] The evil Lord Voldemort, the schoolboy wizard's great enemy, splits his soul into small pieces and hides them in objects around the world. Until all of them can be found and destroyed, he cannot be killed. In the same way, the process of securitization had left "toxic" subprime assets, many of them worthless, on the books of banks across the world. Nobody knew where they were, and until they were identified, all banks were suspect. Fragments of the soul of Lord Voldemortgage might lurk on any balance sheet. And with that, trust broke down. The collateral offered in return for a loan might prove worthless, so banks simply stopped lending to each other.

This drama played out in the "repo" market, where many banks increasingly chose to finance themselves. In repo transactions, banks borrow just for one night, in return for putting up bonds that they promise to repurchase (or "repo") the next day. Investment banks relied on such funding, meaning they could run out of money altogether if denied repo funds for only a few days. That seemed a real possibility. Banks would ask for funds, put up securities as collateral, and find no takers unless they agreed to pay ever higher interest rates. The result was that banks were starved of funds.[3]

Once this basic trust dried up, so did the market for commercial paper—investors were not willing to lend to big companies either, even over short terms. This was particularly true of asset-backed commercial paper with debt as collateral, as all debt securities were now suspect. As large companies often rely on commercial paper to fund their payroll every two weeks, even a brief market interruption could cause disaster.

These dull markets are like the plumbing of the financial system. Nobody cares about them until something breaks and causes a flood. Then, suddenly, nothing is more important. Two indicators, or symptoms, revealed the problem to the outside world. One was the yield paid on Treasury bills. These are bonds issued by the U.S. Treasury that will be repaid within three months—the lowest risk investments that exist. When investors lose their faith in other low-risk investments like commercial paper, they tend to move to T-bills. The extra buying pushes down their yields, so a fall in T-bill yields shows that trust is breaking down.

Secondly, there is the gap between the rate at which banks lend to each other (known as LIBOR, short for the London Inter-Bank Offer Rate) and the T-bill rate—a measure known as the TED spread. LIBOR is usually slightly higher, reflecting the slight extra risk that goes with lending to a big bank rather than to the government. The gap between the two tends to be very stable over time, and if it widens, this shows that banks' trust in each other is breaking down. As Figure 19.1 shows, trust was unnaturally strong during the years of the Great Moderation and broke down completely in the months following August 2007 (see Figure 19.2). Cramer was merely voicing the fears already apparent in money market prices—and throwing down the gauntlet to the Fed.

The plumbing crisis came to a head in the sleepy last week of August when Countrywide Financial, which originated some 17 percent of all U.S. mortgages, found it hard to sell commercial paper. The market guessed that it was sitting on terrible losses and refused to buy (or in other words, refused to give it a short-term loan). A Countrywide collapse would have caused unthinkable damage to the economy, so throughout the summer, as its crisis deepened, its shares moved in almost perfect alignment with Treasury bills. Any sign that things looked worse for Countrywide sparked a race for T-bills. On the morning of August 16, it failed to raise funds by means of commercial paper. Its shares fell 40 percent in hours, while the yield on the three-month T-bill fell by half a percentage point—an enormous move in this market—as investors fled anything that might have mortgages for collateral.[4] This was the worst market seizure since LTCM.

Cooler heads, however, were playing a game of chicken. Named after the scene in James Dean's *Rebel Without a Cause* where two young rebels accelerate their cars toward the edge of the cliff, the loser of a chicken game is the one who swerves first. The problem is that the winner might kill himself in the process of winning. Did the Fed have the nerve to let Countrywide go down? By buying stocks, traders bet that the banking system was in such jeopardy that the central bank would have to swerve. The S&P 500 bounced in the last hours of the afternoon and closed higher for the day.

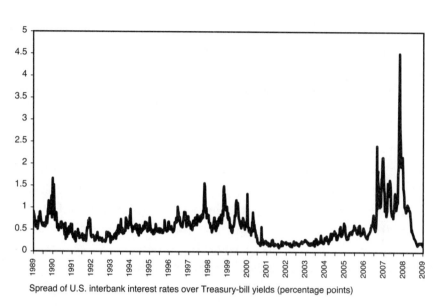

Spread of U.S. interbank interest rates over Treasury-bill yields (percentage points)

Figure 19.1 *The "TED Spread"—the gauge of trust*

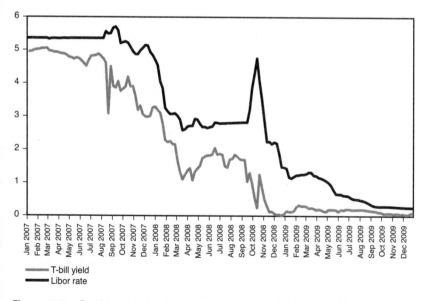

T-bill yield
Libor rate

Figure 19.2 *Breakdown in trust: T-bill yields collapse while bank lending rates soar*

The next morning, the Fed announced that it was cutting the discount rate at which it lends to banks from 6.25 to 5.75 percent (prompting Countrywide stock to rise 60 percent in four hours), and it followed through with another rate cut at its next meeting. Traders rejoiced that the "Greenspan Put" had been replaced by the "Bernanke Put." In the two months following the nadir of the Countrywide crisis, the S&P 500 rose 14 percent.

How did this happen? Investors were following the script from the LTCM crisis nine years earlier and assuming that the problems were restricted to Countrywide, just as they had been restricted to LTCM a decade earlier. Once more, lower rates from the Fed prompted money to gush to the parts of the economy that were healthiest and least in need of help—which in 1999 had been tech stocks.

The equivalent of tech stocks in 2007 was emerging markets. MSCI's emerging markets index hit a bottom on August 16 and then went on a ten-week rally. By October 31, Halloween, it had risen 40 percent, while the BRICs rocketed up by 57 percent. Western appetite for risk, more than anything else, drove them upward. In the words of the Prince song, investors were trying to "party like it's 1999." The Fed had been challenged and had blinked. In this way, a funding crisis for a Californian mortgage-lender turned into a boon for companies in Brazil, Russia, India, and China. And if anyone thought this was sustainable, they were wrong. World markets were now critically vulnerable to a run on the banks—and the banks were poised for just such a run.

In Summary

- Banking, even when carried out by money markets, relies on trust. Without it, the whole financing system is endangered.
- Cheap rates can bail out money markets, but at the cost of inflating speculative bubbles in sectors that do not need help.

Chapter 20

Bank Runs

"With this one piece of legislation, the fear which operated so efficiently to transmit weakness was dissolved. As a result the grievous defect of the old system, by which failure begot failure, was cured."[1]

J.K. Galbraith, on deposit insurance

Market financing of banks makes them vulnerable to "bank runs"—when depositors lose confidence in them and pull out their funds. The run on the UK's Northern Rock showed that bank runs could still happen. The runs on Wall Street's "shadow banks" and then on Bear Stearns were more deadly because they had investments throughout the global financial system—a run on a single bank could burst bubbles across the world.

On the night of September 13, 2007, Robert Peston, the BBC's business correspondent,[2] went on national television news to announce that Northern Rock, a large mortgage lender, was receiving "emergency financial support" from the Bank of England. It was a big scoop, as the deal to help Northern Rock was not meant to be public until the following morning. Peston was careful not to exaggerate. In his second sentence, he said, "this does not mean that the bank is in danger of going bust," and he even added that there was "no reason for people with Northern Rock savings accounts to panic."[3]

The next morning, people with Northern Rock savings accounts panicked. The bank's website went down under the weight of enquiries. Queues started to form around Northern Rock branches. As the bank emphasized online accounts, it had relatively few branches, so spectacularly long queues formed at each one. They did this even though there was generous deposit insurance. The government guaranteed the first £2,000 in every account and 90 percent up to £30,000. Only amounts in excess of this amount, rather higher than most people should keep in bank deposits, were at risk.

The incident shattered confidence in the UK's financial regulation and in the Labour government. It demonstrated herd dynamics in action: After confidence dwindles, in a crowd setting, it disappears. The UK responded by raising the insurance on Northern Rock accounts without limit, meaning that its depositors could treat themselves as having lent to the UK government. It was then taken over by the government and when no buyer came forward, it was nationalized.

This was the biggest bank run in a developed country since the Depression. Deposit insurance, by removing depositors' fear that they could lose their savings, had made runs a thing of the past—just as extra deposit insurance ended the run on the Rock. It did not stop banks from making stupid loans, but it did protect them from suddenly losing deposits—at least until Northern Rock—and this made the system more secure. In return, the premiums they paid and the extra scrutiny they received tended to limit growth. In the 1930s, and again now, this seems a good trade-off, but the concept had detractors.

Before the Depression, bank runs and failures were common. In theory, this is because depositors' ability to take their money out is a kind of monitoring system. A run is a brutal form of market discipline—and markets are capable of unsentimental judgments in a way that human regulators never are. Deposit insurance was a kind of moral hazard. Thus bankers were against it in the 1930s, with one senior executive complaining that "the competence of bankers is not an insurable risk."[4]

Market discipline's problem is that it can be unfair and irrational. Regulators can avoid the irrational panic that followed Peston's report on the BBC. Because markets involve group behavior, they cannot. Further, bank runs can mete out their justice on healthy banks. Banks rely on short-term funding from deposits while lending over longer terms. This is an inherently unstable model, so it is always possible for a bank to become illiquid—to run out of the ready cash provided to it by depositors—without necessarily being insolvent (which means that its assets are worth less than its liabilities, so it cannot settle all its outstanding loans and debts). Thus relying on market discipline is dangerous. While in theory it is appealing to require investors to do all the due diligence on savings accounts, experience suggests that this will not work. In practice, deposit insurance is one state intervention worth making.

The problem is that commercial banks found ways around deposit insurance while investment banks, which were never covered by deposit insurance in the first place, voluntarily chose to finance themselves in a way that made them vulnerable to a run. A critical example was the structured investment vehicle (SIV) that started as a ruse to help banks generate higher returns for their clients while staying within the regulatory rules. SIVs, like mini-banks, lend long-term by buying mortgage-backed securities and borrow in the short-term by issuing commercial paper backed by those mortgage-backed securities. The profits flow back to the bank, but the risks do not appear on the balance sheet.

As trust collapsed in the money markets, SIVs lost the ability to borrow, giving regulators a dilemma. Citigroup, which used the model more than any other bank, at one point ran SIVs worth $80 billion.[5] As with Northern Rock, its creditors (in this case buyers of commercial paper rather than depositors), went on strike. The logical next step, if the SIVs' creditors refused to lend them more money, was to embark on "fire sales" of their mortgage-backed bonds and force the market lower.

In Europe, banks started to bail out their SIVs and put them on their balance sheets. In the United States, the Treasury tried to organize a "Super SIV," which would have raised loans from the commercial paper market and then bought up securities from other distressed SIVs. But the bank run carried on apace. Many believed that the Super SIV was merely a rescue operation to spare Citigroup from taking losses and the fund never got off the ground.[6]

It was this invisible bank run that brought world markets down from their all-time high. Both the MSCI World and Emerging Markets Indices set their records on the ominous date of October 31, 2007—Halloween. The next morning brought a report by Meredith Whitney, then an analyst for CIBC World Markets in New York, that Citi would need to raise $30 billion in new capital to cover the costs of the assets it would have to write off.[7] That implied issuing new shares (and diluting the share price) and cutting the dividend.

Citi's shares dropped 7 percent the next day. UBS, the biggest Swiss bank, fell more than 5 percent on similar concerns, while the S&P 500 financial index, covering the shares of big banks, dropped 4.6 percent, its worst fall in four years on the worst day's trading since the Shanghai Surprise eight months earlier.

How could worries about Citi's SIVs end the rally in emerging markets? If there were a run on Citigroup, the world's most interconnected bank, the logic went, then there would soon be fewer funds available for emerging markets—and the implications for the U.S. economy itself, the world's buyer of last resort, looked ugly. Moreover, many investors had to meet claims from their creditors, and that meant selling the emerging markets while they still showed a profit. Interconnectivity spread the crisis across the globe.

Four months later, another bank run took the crisis to a new level of severity. Bear Stearns was the fifth largest investment bank on Wall Street. Aggressively reliant on short-term funding through the money markets, it had not raised any extra capital in the autumn of 2007. Now it was too late. The essential problem, yet again, was that Bear was holding assets of dubious value. The market lost its confidence in them, so investors in the money markets refused to lend Bear the short-term funds it needed to keep operating. Meanwhile, many hedge funds used Bear Stearns as their "prime broker," meaning it was the bank where they deposited their funds. In the event of a bankruptcy, their funds might be stuck there, so they pulled their money out.

There was an added element to this bank run. Many bought protection against a Bear Stearns default, using credit default swaps. The more investors who bought credit default swaps, the higher the cost of protection would be. This raised the price at which Bear Stearns could borrow, which was bound to be higher if the insurance cost more. But this was not just about protection. To buy a Bear Stearns credit default swap was to place a bet that it would go bust. There was no need to hold any Bear Stearns debt. Instead, it was like buying an insurance policy on a house you do not own—you were not at risk in the first place, but you profit if it burns down.

Hence, traders bought protection as a form of speculative attack. As they piled in, they made it harder for Bear to raise new money. That damaged its share price. Speculators then sold short the stock, making money both as the stock went down and the cost of insurance rose. A falling share price made it more expensive for Bear to raise funds by issuing new equity.

By the night of Thursday, March 13, Bear had only $2 billion in cash left, compared with the $18 billion with which it had started the week, and told its regulators that it would file for bankruptcy the next morning. Instead, in a flurry of action, the politicians arranged a deal that forced Bear Stearns to sell to JP Morgan, a much stronger bank, at a price of $10 per share. Barely a year earlier they had traded for $170 per share. $30 billion in guarantees from the government persuaded JP Morgan to do the deal.[8]

Bear Stearns was not a commercial bank, but the way it funded itself made it prone to an old-fashioned bank run, made more aggressive by short-selling and default swaps. That run removed all control from Bear's managers. Because of Bear's roles lending to hedge funds, holding their accounts, and standing as a counterparty in many credit default swaps, a disorderly demise could have turned into a run on many world markets. Rather than being too *big* to be allowed to fail, it was too *interconnected* to fail.

Rescuing Bear, however, created its own problems. At the worst point of the Bear crisis, the S&P 500 was down more than 20 percent from its peak—a "bear market" in more ways than one. But the hope took hold that Bear had marked the end of the crisis. The response was to buy oil in a bet that contained the seeds of its own destruction.

In Summary

- Deposit insurance almost eliminated bank runs, but money markets found ways around it.
- Investment banks chose to finance themselves in a way—through the repo market—that made them vulnerable to such runs.
- These banks became so interconnected that a run on them could crash numerous other markets—and the run on Bear Stearns showed the dangers.

Chapter 21

Bastille Day: Reflexive Markets

"First, market prices always distort the underlying reality which they are supposed to reflect. The degree of distortion may range from the negligible to the significant. Second, instead of playing a purely passive role in reflecting an underlying reality, financial markets also have an active role: They can affect the so-called fundamentals they are supposed to reflect."

George Soros,[1] explaining the two principles of his theory of markets

---

Synchronized markets warp perception and force politicians and investors alike into historic errors—but eventually collapse under their own contradictions. In 2008, investors bet simultaneously on a banking collapse and an oil spike and caused an inflation scare in the middle of a credit crisis. When it ended, oil, foreign exchange, and stock markets all reversed, setting the scene for collapse.

July 14, Bastille Day, is a day of revolution, and in 2008, it was the moment when the old regime for markets fell. Entering Bastille Day, there had been one way to make money in 2008, which was to bet against Uncle Sam, and particularly against the Fed. The logic: The U.S. financial system was critically wounded and the Federal Reserve had given up any attempt to stave off inflation or to avoid moral hazard. Instead, it would go all out to rescue U.S. banks by cutting rates and doing anything else necessary. The market response to this was so extreme that it forced central banks to fight inflation by raising rates—and thus killed off the rally.

This was a classic example of a "negative feedback loop," or what the investor George Soros calls "reflexivity." By this, Soros means that our perceptions of the world, as expressed through buying and selling, can change the world itself. Once markets become reflexive, they reflect flawed perceptions rather than a prior "reality"—but the market's version of "reality" is no less real because of that. The reflexive events of the summer of 2008 are the textbook case of how synchronized markets have evolved so that they can force policy mistakes and damage the economy.

The chain of events went as follows. After the Bear Stearns rescue and the rate cut that followed it, traders reasoned that the Fed had given up on its currency. So they bet the dollar would decline. A great way to do this, as the experience of the 1970s had shown, was to buy oil, which would retain its value as the dollar dropped. They could also directly sell the dollar in favor of other currencies on the foreign exchange market. Belief in big ideas like "decoupling" and the BRICs made the idea seem all the better.

If hedge funds really wanted to profit, however, they could be more aggressive by selling short the shares of U.S. banks and buying oil. This was a connected bet that the U.S. banks would keep sinking and that the cheap money to save them would weaken the dollar and send money pouring out of the United States. Just like the rally for Internet stocks after the rescue of LTCM, or the rush for the BRICs in 2007, they were betting that cheap money to cure an ailing patient would instead over-stimulate parts of the world economy that were already in robust health.

Returns on this trade were spectacular and are illustrated in Figure 21.1, which shows the returns made by selling short U.S. bank shares and using the money to buy crude oil futures. By July 14, this trade had made a profit of 168 percent for the year. The trend for the rest of the world was only a little more muted. Shorting the broader MSCI World financials index, which includes banks from around the developed world (most of which were exposed to U.S. housing), instead of U.S. banks would have netted 114 percent.

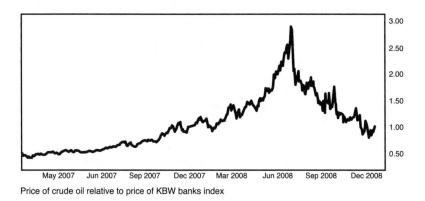

Price of crude oil relative to price of KBW banks index

Figure 21.1 *Betting against Uncle Sam: buy oil, sell banks*

By July, the oil price reached $145 per barrel, having doubled since the previous August, and tripled since the previous January— astonishingly, this happened against a background of declining global demand for oil and rising supply.

The longer term problem with the trade was that it was internally illogical. If the United States was really to fall into the grips of an acute banking crisis, then its economic activity would slow and it would buy less oil. It was the world's biggest oil consumer, so this meant oil would fall, not rise. But the flows of money pushing up oil, in several distinct markets, were so heavy that the price could be taken to an extreme.

This "Sell Uncle Sam" trade put central banks under intolerable pressure. Oil is a big chunk of the consumer baskets on which inflation indexes are based, so rising oil led directly to higher inflation (just as it had done in the 1970s). Now that markets appeared no longer to trust central banks to keep inflation under control, the United States was back on the "oil standard" that had governed its economy in the 1970s. This was reflexivity—by betting on a return to inflation, traders had in a very real way helped inflation come to pass.

A credit crisis would normally lead to deflation. But as oil shot upward, central bankers took their eyes off the credit market and felt forced to declare war on inflation. Indeed, some central bankers virtually declared war on each other.

Central bankers try never to talk about their currency if they can avoid it. But on June 3, speaking by satellite to a conference in Barcelona, Ben Bernanke did just that. He complained of an "unwelcome rise in import prices and consumer price inflation" and said he was "attentive" to the implications that the weak dollar could have for inflation and inflation expectations. When the dollar weakens, import prices rise, and this forces up inflation, so this was an obvious attempt to push the currency higher by talking up its prospects.

Two days later, Jean-Claude Trichet of the European Central Bank (ECB) went one better, virtually promising to raise rates. He announced that he had "markedly higher" new projections for European inflation, that there was a risk of high oil prices leading to a "wage/price spiral" and that "we are in a state of heightened alertness." He also predicted that economic growth would soon hit bottom at 1.5 percent annually and then recover.

A rate rise fought inflation, but it also strengthened the euro even more against the dollar because it raised the rates paid by euro-denominated deposits. So the dollar fell amid chaotic conditions in which many traders took severe losses. If central bankers were worried by inflation, the logic went, it must make sense to buy oil. With markets now helplessly interconnected, oil rose still more, while the sell-off of banks continued apace. Bizarrely, it even implied that the ECB should have cut rates if it really wanted to fight inflation, as a weaker euro might have led to cheaper oil.

This was reflexivity at its most deadly. Once the oil price had risen, whether for "good" reasons or bad, it had real effects on the economy and changed such crucial factors as the interest rates in the world's two biggest economies. Traders bought oil as a sensible hedge against falling interest rates in the United States; but then they bought so much oil that they forced central banks to raise rates instead. Instead of hedging against a bad economic outcome, the rush into oil forced a serious policy mistake and helped to create an economic disaster.

Meanwhile, the other side of the trade, attacking banks, also reached the point of self-destruction. Selling banks short when they desperately needed new capital, much like buying oil to hedge against inflation, was a self-fulfilling prophecy. The latest institutions to fall into trouble were Fannie Mae and Freddie Mac, the pillars of the U.S. mortgage market. It was obvious that they did not have the capital to cover growing losses. They could not borrow more—that was how they had landed in trouble in the first place. But their falling share price meant that they could not raise equity either. Many banks held bonds or stock issued by Fannie and Freddie, so traders sold their stock as well.

In this way, the markets created a "reality" of spiking oil prices and failing U.S. financial institutions. But on Bastille Day, the "Sell Uncle Sam" trade collapsed under its own weight. It had never made sense, even if for a few months it had generated a lot of money. Now multiple actors in multiple markets across the world made sure that a new reality imposed itself.

In the first week of July, the ECB said it would not raise rates further, so the successful bid to bounce central banks into pushing up the dollar was no longer working. In the United States, on July 13, the government guaranteed the bonds of Fannie Mae and Freddie Mac. They would not be allowed to go under. Banks enjoyed a rebound.

Simultaneously, on the other side of the world, China sent terror through the markets by stopping its currency from rising. For the previous three years, it had allowed its currency, the renminbi, to rise gradually by 20 percent against the dollar in a managed and steady upward straight line. This redressed the global imbalances that so alarmed the U.S. without causing the disruption of a major currency crisis, and it also helped guard against Chinese inflation. But the Chinese suddenly decided to stop the renminbi from gaining against the dollar, while allowing it to keep rising against all other currencies, bar the Japanese yen.

All other things equal, this action would cause the dollar to rise—if it was pegged against renminbi, and the renminbi rose against the euro, then logically the dollar would do the same thing. And a rise in the dollar would reduce the price of oil, which must at this point have been crippling for Chinese industry, as oil and the dollar were in lockstep. Whether or not this was a deliberate aim of the Chinese authorities, a fall in oil price resulted, and their actions contributed to it.

With the authorities of Europe, the U.S., and China all apparently determined that the dollar should rise, on Bastille Day it duly did, leaping against all currencies bar the yen and putting at a disadvantage the many investors who had bet against the dollar by buying stocks outside the U.S. It kept gaining as that money came home to the U.S., and by the end of the year the euro had fallen from its lofty perch of $1.59 all the way to $1.25.

The rise in U.S. banks' share prices and the gain in the dollar inflicted losses on investors who had piled into oil. And so, on Bastille

Day, they took profits. With no news from the oil industry to push it, oil started a precipitate fall, dropping all the way to $35 per barrel by December. And extraordinarily, any trader who had kept on his "Bet Against Uncle Sam" trade of shorting U.S. banks and buying oil would have lost money for the year—despite the epic spike in mid-year, oil suffered a bigger fall for the year than did the shares of U.S. banks.

As the oil price tumbled, the market abruptly lost its fear of inflation. Faith in the BRICs, commodities, and "decoupling" went with it. The many traders who had survived the mayhem in the financial markets by betting on the BRICs were caught out and left sitting on losses. Deprived of what had been virtually the only way to make money in 2008, they had to embark on the painful process of "deleveraging"—selling what assets they could, to raise money to pay off their debts. That soon had its own devastating consequences.

In Summary

- Markets are reflexive—they can create their own reality.
- The run on the dollar and U.S. banks and the oil price spike of 2008 forced serious policy errors by central banks and forced governments across the world to respond.
- The spike was the result of moral hazard, cheap money, and hedge funds' propensity to push trends too far.
- Lessons for the future are that the world remains on the "oil standard" and that rallies that so utterly contradict economic reality should be avoided.

Chapter 22

Lessons from Lehman

"So I'm the schmuck?"

Richard Fuld, CEO of Lehman Brothers, on learning a rescue deal had fallen through[1]

The Lehman Brothers bankruptcy triggered a market meltdown. The U.S. government tried to show that it would no longer bail out risk-taking at every turn, only to find that it had left it too late to do so. As a result, money market funds suffered a "bank run," which paralyzed markets across the world.

The events of September 14 and September 15, 2008, Wall Street's lost weekend, passed into popular culture almost the moment they happened. It was the weekend when Lehman Brothers, the fourth largest U.S. investment bank, filed for bankruptcy; Merrill Lynch, the third largest, sold itself to Bank of America; and American International Group, the world's biggest insurer, begged for government support. Within months, whole books had already been published about it. Movies will doubtless follow. As the principals' version of events has steadily reached the public, it has become clear that this succession of events might easily have been different.

But how did Lehman get into such a state and how did its fall trigger the most synchronized financial crisis in history? Its bankruptcy was part of a belated United States attempt to deal with the moral hazard that it had allowed to build up since the bailout of the Long-Term Capital Management hedge fund in 1998, only to find out that it was too late to do so because moral hazard was so entrenched that it could not be uprooted without triggering disaster. The replacement of insured banks with money markets had created the risk of a bank run. In addition, the money markets provided leverage to finance deals, meaning that any such run could swiftly create multiple disasters in multiple markets.

The first key event of the Lehman debacle came on Sunday, September 7, when the U.S. Treasury secretary Hank Paulson nationalized Fannie Mae and Freddie Mac, taking action before it was utterly necessary. Confidence in Fannie and Freddie was oozing away, but there was no particular reason to expect a move that weekend. Many, including the companies' own executives, were surprised that it happened.

Debt-holders were protected. Foreign governments had bought Fannie and Freddie's bonds in the belief that they were as safe as Treasury bonds and the United States was politically bound to honor these obligations. But shareholders, including "preferred" shareholders who had superior rights to holders of ordinary shares, were wiped out. Many small U.S. commercial banks held the preferred stock, which they had treated as a safe investment, so this knocked their already precarious finances. Paulson was trying to show that he was at last stamping out the moral hazard created by the LTCM rescue and he succeeded. The perceived risks of holding bank stocks escalated.

The next question was who would be next? The obvious answer was Lehman, the smallest remaining investment bank. It was sitting on credit losses, like Bear Stearns before it, and it directly owned a big portfolio of commercial real estate, which appeared likely to suffer losses. As with Bear Stearns, traders shorted the stock while buying default insurance. This did not cause Lehman's demise, but it did determine the timing.

Lehman was incapable of opening for trading on September 15. If a bank had been found to play the role JP Morgan had taken with Bear, a rescue would probably have happened—but amid much confusion and miscommunication that dramatic weekend, no buyer came forward.[2] Therefore, Lehman was left to go bankrupt.

This decision led to disaster. But a look at what happened next suggests that rescuing Lehman in September 2008 would merely have postponed the reckoning—the system was primed for collapse. Beyond their belief that the financial system would benefit from a demonstration that taking bad risks could have consequences, Paulson and many of his colleagues appear to have believed that companies would have contingency plans in place, as it was six months after the fall of Bear Stearns.

But they did not have such a plan. Hedge funds who banked with Lehman found their money frozen, hamstringing them. Unable to raise cash, they sold their other assets, causing havoc in previously unconnected markets.

True panic arrived after New York markets closed on Tuesday, when the Reserve Fund, which had pioneered money market funds four decades earlier, admitted that its Primary Fund held $785 million in now worthless bonds issued by Lehman. This was far too big a gap for the management company to make up, so the fund announced that it could only pay its investors 97 cents for each dollar they had invested. In other words, it "broke the buck." Only weeks earlier, Reserve's chairman had told his investors that he was "boring [them] into a sound sleep." Adding insult to injury, investors would also have to wait at least seven days for their money.

Almost simultaneously, the government announced that it was lending $85 billion to AIG and taking a controlling stake in return—another virtual nationalization. This was terrifying because of AIG's role in using credit default swaps to guarantee debts. Effectively, its insurance allowed most of the big banks in Europe to pretend that the debts they held on their balance sheets were worth far more than they could fetch in the market. Without AIG's insurance, the credit investments sitting in European bank vaults and in U.S. investment banks like Goldman Sachs would no longer be rated AAA and would fall in value. Under the Basel regulations, that would mean that the banks would have to find more capital to back them. Thus, failure by AIG would jeopardize the solvency of the European banking system.

Financiers understood the implications better than the public at large. These events implied a risk that customers would put their bank cards into ATM machines and no money would come out, that companies would fail to pay their workers the next week, and that credit cards would cease to work. The economic consequences were close to unimaginable. If AIG needed so much help, they understood that such an inconceivable disaster was close.

All of this triggered outright panic when markets opened on Wednesday. Investors wanted out of money market funds, while the money market funds themselves wanted out of anything that did not have a U.S. government guarantee. The result was a market bank run. That week, the money held in institutional money market funds fell by $176 billion—and the assets of funds not restricted solely to government securities fell by $239 billion. The stampede to buy Treasury bills pushed their rate down to 0.02 percent, its lowest since 1941. Security had never been so expensive. In such conditions, no company could fund itself.

It was now clear that money funds' repeated interventions to stop any fund from "breaking the buck" had convinced investors that they were no riskier than bank accounts. A small loss of 3 percent was enough to shatter that belief. Money market funds had to a great extent gained their prominent position because, unlike banks, they did not have to pay for deposit insurance. The run after Lehman showed that they were just as susceptible to runs as banks had been before deposit insurance.

And indeed, the government's response to the money market fund run and to the AIG crisis was effectively to offer deposit insurance after the event. They paid AIG's contracts in full (involving the payment of more than $22 billion to banks) and offered federal guarantees on money market funds.

This was a retreat from the attempt to take a stand against moral hazard. But investors' reaction in the days after Lehman showed that the moral hazard in the system had grown to become overwhelming. Fannie and Freddie's preferred stockholders, Lehman's counterparties, the Reserve Fund's clients, and AIG's clients had all assumed that their investments were guaranteed. Such comfortable assumptions were so widespread that allowing any more failures would have made the situation far worse; Lehman's demise proved that it was already too late to deal with moral hazard, and that the market had grown too reliant on its belief in government help.

That left politicians no choice but to revive confidence by bailing out reckless institutions and re-injecting moral hazard into the system. This would provide just the cheap money and overconfidence needed to inflate another bubble. Investors knew this.

The end of that September week saw one of the biggest rebounds ever as the government's response took shape. Short-selling was banned and then Paulson announced a plan to spend $700 billion buying up toxic debt. Stock markets ended the week higher than they had started. That rebound showed the market trusted its politicians. The next question was whether that faith was justified.

In Summary

Lehman's collapse proved:

- It was too interconnected to be allowed to fail.
- Money market funds were vulnerable to a bank run.
- There was too much moral hazard embedded in markets to risk letting a big bank fail. It forced governments to re-create moral hazard.

Chapter 23

Politics and Institutions

"Now, as through history, financial capacity and political perspicacity are inversely correlated.... So inaction will be advocated in the present even though it means deep trouble in the future. Here, at least equally with communism, lies the threat to capitalism. It is what causes men who know that things are going quite wrong to say that things are fundamentally sound."

J.K Galbraith, from *The Great Crash 1929*, written in 1954

Confidence in political institutions is vital to markets, and usually taken for granted. Once lost, it is expensive to replace. When Congress voted down the TARP bailout plan and then the European Union showed itself incapable of coordinating a response to runs on European banks, markets lost their confidence in governments—and the super-bubble burst.

Traders on the floor of the New York Stock Exchange do not spend much time watching politics. They are much more concerned by stock prices. But that changed on September 29, 2008.

The United States had just lived through a week of political drama. Figures on both left and right in Congress had principled reasons to dislike Henry Paulson's so-called TARP—Troubled Assets Relief Plan. The idea was to buy up troubled mortgage-backed securities, and thereby ease pressure on the banks holding them. But for those on the left, it was an anathema to bail out Wall Street when Main Street America was suffering. Those on the right believed the market should be allowed to take its course. And they were being asked to ratify a $700 billion bailout a month before they faced re-election. Barack Obama and John McCain, the two presidential candidates, both took part in highly publicized talks while the incumbent president, George W. Bush, looking as pale as a ghost, made a national broadcast to sell the deal.

Eventually, a compromise emerged, and leaders of both parties in the House decided to put it to a vote. Traders assumed that they would not have done so, with so much at stake, unless they were sure they had the votes to pass it. And in any case, it seemed clear that politicians had no choice but to hold their noses and pass the legislation.

As the debate in the House of Representatives started that Monday morning, trading on the exchange floor was desultory. Politicians were unsettling background noise. As they moved to a vote to give the Treasury $700 billion for a bailout, Wall Street trading ground to a halt. The votes slowly tallied at the top of the television screen—and, unbelievably, the Nays accumulated faster than the Yeas. They were still ahead when the vote ended. Television commentators dickered over whether this was the end for the bailout, but the traders reacted in the only way that made sense. They sold.

Normally the bulk of trades in Wall Street come at the beginning and end of the day, as traders reconcile the orders they have taken from outside. Even the biggest news cannot disrupt that pattern. But on this day, the dealing that took place in a few frantic minutes after midday swamped anything else seen all day.

In "raw" points terms the Dow Jones Industrial Average ended down exactly 777 points, the worst day in its history. But the total market value wiped out in the United States alone came to about

$1.5 trillion, or nearly double the amount that Congress had decided not to spend on the toxic assets problem. As most of the U.S. stock market ultimately belongs to taxpayers, the attempt to safeguard voters' personal budgets had, at least initially, been hugely counterproductive.

The problem for the markets was not the money involved, or even the toxic assets, *per se*. The TARP plan was muddled, and many thought that any rescue plan should be very differently structured. Rather, it was that Congress had unintentionally shown them that they could not rely on politicians to get their house in order, to take action when it was needed, or even to pay attention to critical financial issues. The institutions on which the markets rely for order simply did not function. Weak institutions like this had always been perceived as part of the risk of investing in emerging markets; now American political institutions were revealed to be no stronger.

Bringing the issue to the vote, only to see it go down, was much worse for confidence than doing nothing at all. Art Cashin, known as the dean of the trading floor, where he had worked for 47 years, commented that it was as though the traders were on a ship in a storm— and had suddenly seen the officers and crew in a pitched battle with each other.[1]

This is what was truly toxic. Finally passing the TARP (which happened four days later with the aid of huge and unrelated amounts of government largesse, or "pork," directed at the districts of prominent "no" voters) did not correct it. It was beyond doubt that the politicians did not understand the situation and did not have their act together. And investors around the world focused on the risk that other politicians would handle the situation no better than the Americans.

The United States had been around for more than two centuries. Its institutions were stable. What chance, then, was there for the European Union? A group of different countries, speaking different languages, and in some cases, harboring deep historic grudges against each other, had to grapple with problems just as difficult. On the same day that Congress voted down the TARP, Ireland stemmed what looked like a nascent bank run by announcing far more generous deposit insurance. It quintupled the amount of each deposit covered from €20,000 to €100,000, making it by far the most generous insurance scheme among the countries that used the euro. The next day it went further, making a blanket guarantee of all Irish deposits. They had a big incentive to do this, as Ireland's banking system was blatantly "too big to fail," with assets four times greater than the country's GDP. For comparison, U.S. bank assets were exactly equal to GDP.[2]

Anxious Europeans started to pull their funds from local banks and move them to Ireland. This was easily done with Internet banking, as all the accounts were denominated in euros. Hence funds flowed out of the continent's biggest banks. Leaders tried to agree on a common standard for deposit insurance with a €350 billion price tag, an idea that appeared to originate from France, but by the weekend the talks were mired in acrimony.

Traditional European enmities bubbled up once more. On Thursday of that week, Angela Merkel, Germany's chancellor, depth-charged the talks, saying: "The federal government cannot and will not issue a blank check for all banks, regardless of whether they behave in a responsible manner or not."[3] Then on Sunday, as the panic deepened, she announced that the German government would do just that, guaranteeing all private German bank accounts.[4]

This rammed home that Europe's politicians could not speak with one voice. In a crisis, when decisions had to be made swiftly, its big and cumbersome institutions did not allow a coherent response—especially when Europe's banks were obviously even more bloated, and would be even harder to rescue, than U.S. banks. Confidence in politicians was lost.

Like a functioning banking system, a coherent political system tends to be taken for granted. People notice it only when it goes missing. But good governance matters. The lack of strong institutions or politicians that investors could trust was a key reason why emerging markets were cheaper than developed markets in the first place. Now it turned out that developed markets were no better. At the end of September 2008, markets suddenly lost the "stability dividend" that decades of stable government in the United States and Europe had given to markets.

Recovery would be impossible until that confidence could be bought back. And the price of buying back confidence would prove much higher than the original $700 billion price tag on the TARP.

In Summary:

- Coherent government institutions are a necessary condition for properly functioning markets.
- Lost confidence in U.S. and European governments' capability to respond to the banking crisis provided the final catalyst for the crash of 2008.

Chapter 24

The Paradox of Diversification

Jon Stewart: "My mother is 75 and she bought into the idea that long-term investing is the way to go. And guess what?"

Jim Cramer: "It didn't work."

Interview on Comedy Central's *The Daily Show with Jon Stewart*, March 11, 2009

October 2008 saw virtually every kind of asset collapse together, in truly unprecedented fashion. This inflicted losses on most investors around the world and showed that they need a new way to mitigate risk.

By Monday, October 6, 2008, all reason for optimism had been exhausted—there was a run on banks, governments evidently could not deal with it, and markets were wildly overvalued after decades of moral hazard and herding behavior by investors. The result was the markets' most disastrous week ever. It set all the investment orthodoxies on their heads and proved that markets across the world had been caught in a synchronized bubble.

As markets opened that Monday, the S&P 500 stood at 1099.23. By Friday morning, it was at 839.8, down 23.5 percent. At that point, it was the worst week for the U.S. stock market on record, including the bear market following the 1929 crash.

More remarkable was that it was indiscriminate. MSCI's EAFE Index, covering developed markets outside the United States, fell 22.4 percent for the week; its World index fell 22.5 percent; and its emerging markets index fell 21.3 percent. Its BRIC Index, where investors could allegedly "decouple" from these problems, fell 21.6 percent. With total synchronicity, virtually all world markets lost one-fifth of their value during the week.

Even within markets, the sell-off did not discriminate—just look at the equal-weighted version of the S&P 500, in which each stock accounts for 0.2 percent of the index (unlike the standard index that is concentrated in the biggest stocks). The equal-weighted index should be better protected in a sell-off after a bubble in certain sectors or stocks. In the years after the Internet bust, it gained while the main S&P fell.

But in 2008, the average stock fell even more than the main index. The equal-weighted index beat the main S&P throughout the rally of 2003–2007, but when disaster struck it fell by more, ending 48.5 percent down from its peak. The phenomenon was global. The MSCI World Index of developed world stocks fell 49 percent during the sell-off, the same as the capitalization-weighted version of the index. By the calculations of GMO, the Boston-based fund managers, the main index should suffer a fall this severe about once every 100 years; it should happen to the equal-weighted index only once every 34,000 years.[1]

When a bubble bursts, it is because it is overvalued. But overvaluation implies that the assets in the bubble are overvalued *with respect to something else*. In this case, every asset that bore any element of risk came down simultaneously. Rather than going somewhere else, the value simply evaporated because it should never have existed in the first place. Markets had grasped that there was more risk in the planet than prices had reflected.

All the asset classes now tied to equities came down with equal ferocity. Over the week, the Australian dollar fell 21.4 percent against the Japanese yen. In other words, the carry trade had collapsed, and the losses traders took on the carry trade were virtually equal to the losses they took on stocks. As U.S. investors made forced sales and repatriated their money, they bought dollars, pushing all other currencies down.

As for commodities, oil fell 16.8 percent that week, continuing the epic slide that had started on Bastille Day. Industrial metals shed 15.6 percent (part of a 64.9 percent fall since their peak in the spring). The cost of hiring a container ship, as measured by the Baltic Dry Index and a proxy for world trade, dropped 26 percent.

Even the assets that should be safe havens during market carnage suffered falls. Gold, traditionally the ultimate refuge from volatility elsewhere, rose more than 11 percent early in the week, but lost it all in a sell-off that Friday. Bonds roughly held their value for the week, but there was no great rush to take money out of currency carry trades, commodities, or stocks and put it in bonds. That would have shown up in rising bond prices. Instead, one-fifth of the wealth that had on paper existed in these assets evaporated.

Research from Research Affiliates, the investment company run by the former academic Rob Arnott, tracked 16 different asset classes, including government and corporate debt, equities, loans, and commodities from around the world. In September 2008, all fell except for long-dated U.S. government bonds (which gained 0.4 percent). In October, all of them fell together, and a portfolio equally weighted among all 16 asset classes would have lost 14.4 percent that month—an almost inconceivable event. Even in August 1998, the month of the LTCM meltdown and the closest previous approach to such a correlated meltdown, six asset classes had shown a profit.[2]

This collapse was the ultimate proof that different asset classes, many of which had only opened to investors after financial innovations of the last decade, had come to reinforce each other. The value of each was not contingent on real-world conditions as much as valuations in other markets. This was the ultimate consequence of the herd-like behavior that the investment industry had encouraged for decades; the herd finally stomped over all of the world's markets.

This blew up investors' most basic notions about diversification and long-term returns. Under the academic orthodoxy that had developed over the previous half-century, diversification is about balancing different asset classes. The correlations between these different assets are assumed to be relatively stable over time; that was why investors hunted for new uncorrelated asset classes in the first place.

If markets are not driven by the same flows and prices are not set in reference to other markets, then diversifying your investments by dividing the world into asset classes or geographies should indeed reduce risks. But now that money travels so easily among them, this is plainly not the case. Traders thought they had made several uncorrelated trades, but in fact they had made the same bet—that the United States was in trouble but "decoupled" emerging markets would be fine—many times over.

All were exposed to the same risks—that money would be withdrawn quickly ("liquidity risk" in the jargon) and that the big rise in commodity prices would end. The crash demonstrated what might be called a new "paradox of diversification"; the more investors bought in to assets on the assumption that they were not correlated, the more they tended to become correlated.

In the future, it would make more sense to divide the world by risk. If an investment is not prone to the same risks as the others you already hold, then buying it will reduce your overall risk. If it is subject to exactly the same risk, then buying it is pointless, even if it is in a different asset class or country. Rather than balance between stocks and bonds, for example, it might be better to balance the risks of inflation and deflation, which both affect stocks and bonds. Diversification itself is as good an idea as ever. You should not put all your eggs in one basket. But in the globalized world, you can put your egg into a different country and still find that it is in the same basket.

Further, the point of a risk is that you do not know in advance if you will be paid for taking it. It cannot be gauged with precision—so the very concept of risk argues for leaving greater margin for error—and it does not lie in correlations between asset classes. Rather, risk management should be about guarding against conditions that could cause those correlations to change.

Another core notion must also be rethought. Ever since the 1950s, the cult of the equity had held sway, backed by both theory and experience. In theory, investors get their profits in return for taking a risk. That risk means that in the short term, returns on equities are volatile. But in the long term, they will get a premium for taking that risk so that equities will outperform safer investments, such as bonds. When teaching valuation, business schools typically assume that this "premium" will be about 7 percent each year.

Exhaustive historical studies show that equities easily beat bonds over the very long run. Compounded over decades, the gap is astronomical. Over the twentieth century, according to research by London Business School, U.S. equities rose at 10.1 percent per year, compared to a 4.8 percent rise for bonds, and a 3.2 percent rise for inflation. Compounded over the century, that meant that $1 in stocks in 1900 became $16,797 in 2000, compared to $119 for bonds. Thanks to inflation, you needed $24 to maintain the buying power of one 1900 dollar. A pound invested in UK stocks did almost as well, turning into £16,160, but UK inflation was roughly double that of the United States.[3]

Thus the premium equities paid over bonds was robust and high. The London Business School study covered 16 countries from 1900 to 2005 and suggested the extra return on equities each year was 6.1 percent—almost as high as the business school guesstimate.[4] So pension funds, and individuals egged on by advertisers, allocated ever more to equities, safe in the knowledge that in the long-run they would do best.

Such faith in long-term equity outperformance made stocks more expensive. Since 1954, the dividend yield on equities had been less than the yield on bonds. That aligned with the orthodoxy that bonds needed to pay a higher yield because equities would rise more in the long-term. But in December 2008, as equities crashed, that assumption came to an end, as dividend yields rose above bond yields.

The comforting long-term averages had concealed another lesson of history: that stocks can do worse than inflation for very long periods. During the twentieth century, all but three countries outside the United States had at least one period of at least 20 years in which equities failed to beat inflation. Developed countries like Japan, Italy, and Germany all went for periods of about half a century in which equities lost money.[5] The assumption that the "long-term" would always bail out equities was always a lazy one.

In February 2009, after the correlated crash, this was proved conclusively. Anyone who started investing in February 1969—when baby boomers were joining the workforce and starting to save—would find 40 years later that bonds had done better than stocks.[6] This ran against all the advice boomers had ever received from the investment industry.

Some argue that the 2008 correlated crash was an aberrant event and provided a great opportunity to buy cheap. When stocks recovered in 2009, their yields dropped back below bond yields. But that does not mean these events can be dismissed. The point of investing in a diverse group of assets, rather than just picking a favorite, is to guard against sharp downturns—which may happen just as savers need access to their money. Protesting that this was an extreme event and that correlations can change in extreme conditions misses the point. Diversification is to protect against just such extreme events.

Relying on stocks to win in the long run is also dangerous. Investors persuaded themselves to pile into equities, to the exclusion of bonds, because the long term would always be there to bail them out. History makes it clear that over time stocks have done better than bonds and so it would be foolish to ignore them. But the historical era for which we have the most complete data involved a long period of peace and prosperity as the world recovered from two world wars, abandoned communism, and enjoyed many technological advances. There is no reason to assume that this can be repeated. Relying on stocks to outperform in the long run only makes sense if we know we will live to be 100 years old. This might be a sensible plan for endowments and charities—but not for any individual.

Nothing falls forever. After the disaster, markets picked up. But that recovery started far from Wall Street or the City of London.

In Summary

- Diversification in its traditional form—balancing different asset classes—has failed. After the 2008 collapse, a new form of diversification is needed.
- The way to achieve this is to allocate according to risks, not asset classes.

Part III

The Fearful Rise

Chapter 25

Decoupling

> *"The Great Wall [of China] is evidence of a historical inability of people in this part of the planet to communicate, to confer and jointly determine how best to deploy enormous reserves of human energy and intellect."*
>
> Ryszard Kapuściński, in Travels with Herodotus

The recovery started in emerging markets, breaking the decades-old pattern of following the lead of developed markets. The good news is that the bigger emerging markets had indeed "emerged" with strong institutions; the bad news is that their recovery seems to have been won only with unsustainably cheap money in China.

The week after the synchronized crash, Controladora Comercial Mexicana SAB (Comerci), Mexico's third-largest supermarket chain, filed for bankruptcy. Its Mexican customers were not much worried by the crisis on Wall Street. But Comerci had taken a $1.1 billion loss on currency derivatives it had bought from banks. These protected it against a rise in the peso but exposed it to great losses if the peso went down. As foreign investors desperately reduced their risk and paid down debts, they sold their Mexican investments. In doing so, they sold pesos and bought dollars, inflicting a sudden collapse on the peso. That brought down Comerci, even though it was largely a domestic concern.

This looked like the beginning of a replay of the emerging markets disasters of the 1990s, with an exit of international money leading to a currency crisis and then a debt crisis. Defaults by governments, a true disaster scenario, seemed a real possibility—but did not happen. Instead, emerging markets led the world in a rebound. It is vital to understand how they did this.

Comerci was not alone. Indeed, the spread of the problem showed how indiscriminately international funds had sought out emerging markets. There were losses like this in Brazil, Hong Kong, India, Indonesia, Malaysia, Poland, and Taiwan. According to the International Monetary Fund (IMF), as many as 50,000 emerging markets companies lost money on currency hedges, including 10 percent of Indonesia's exporters and 571 of Korea's smaller exporters. Losses in Brazil were $28 billion, according to the IMF, while in Indonesia they were $3 billion. Mexico and Poland suffered losses of $5 billion each. Sri Lanka's publicly owned Ceylon Petroleum Company lost $600 million, and even the huge Chinese bank Citic Pacific lost $2.4 billion.[1]

The options sold in Korea were known as KIKO (Knock-In, Knock-Out) and protected against a rise in the local currency up to a certain point; at which point they would knock-out, meaning that there was a lid on the protection they offered against a big rise. In the years when the boom in commodities and BRICs pushed emerging market currencies ever upward, this was a great deal. Effectively, companies buying these options from banks had successfully bet that their currency would keep rising. But if the local currency dropped below the rate at which the contracts knocked-in, then the companies were themselves on the hook to compensate the banks who sold them the derivatives. They had effectively let the banks place a bet with them that their currency would fall.

Regulators watched banks' forex positions closely to avoid a repeat of the Mexican crisis in 2004, when Mexican banks had used swaps to take on foreign exchange risk, but they did not keep the same watchful eye on nonfinancial companies like supermarkets or television manufacturers.

The result nearly turned a crisis into a disaster. In the weeks after Lehman, money poured out of emerging markets, pushing their currencies down, in response to the panic in the West. As emerging markets had been at bubble prices months earlier, many foreigners were still sitting on profits, making them all the more anxious to sell. As they sold bonds, so their yields rose, making it more expensive for companies, or governments, to borrow. When companies ran into forex losses, they had to buy dollars, pushing their own currencies down further.

This painful logic was the exact opposite of "decoupling." Far from offering some protection, MSCI indexes showed emerging markets dropping by two-thirds in the 12 months after their peak on Halloween 2007. In doing to, they underperformed the developed world, where the roots of their problem lay, by 26 percent.

Fragile systems and institutions were put under pressure for the first time and were found wanting. Russia had to close its two biggest stock exchanges for several days in September 2008, under the weight of orders. The momentum seemed unstoppable.

But on October 27, that momentum stopped. Emerging markets stocks stopped, wobbled, and then began a rally, even as fresh panics over the banks saw the developed world markets fall to even worse lows (see Figure 25.1). At least as far as their markets were concerned, the emerging markets had at last "decoupled." They hit bottom and started to recover before anyone else. The importance of this cannot be overstated; after a generation when emerging markets had merely offered a more extreme version of what was available in the developed world—doing better when times were good and worse when times were bad—they had finally parted company (see Figure 25.2).

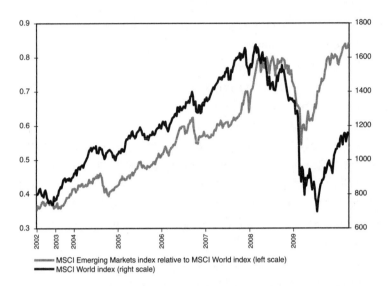

Figure 25.1   *Decoupling? Emerging markets suddenly and briefly parted company from developed markets in October 2008.*

Figure 25.2   *The Brics grow more tightly linked to the developed world.*

What happened? First, the developed world came up with aid. U.S. policymakers knew that big emerging market defaults would ensure a Depression. So on October 30, the Federal Reserve announced "swap lines" of $30 billion each for Brazil, Mexico, Singapore, and South Korea.[2] In English, this meant that they lent dollars to these countries' central banks, which could in turn lend the dollars to domestic companies who were desperate for cash to pay off dollar-denominated loans. Crucially, they could do this without buying dollars on the open market, which would have pushed the local currencies down further. Trying to avoid moral hazard, the Fed restricted aid to systemically important countries with good financial management. It adroitly headed off the dynamic by which currency devaluations had turned into debt crises in the past.

Second, and more important, in late October news filtered out that China had a stimulus plan for its economy. Chinese economic data is carefully managed, but the figures that are hardest to massage looked alarming. For example, electricity generation was falling, implying that the economy might be contracting. Some basic industries, such as the factories making cheap toys and shoes in the Pearl River Delta near Hong Kong, saw dramatic shutdowns amid complaints from workers that factory owners had absconded with their wages.[3]

At the very least, there was a real danger that China's growth would drop below 6 percent per year for the first time since the Tiananmen massacre, 19 years earlier. This would have broken the Communist Party's longstanding compact with the people that it would maintain fast growth. But China was sitting on a huge war chest in the form of its foreign reserves. The hope was that it would reply with devastating force. It did.

The stimulus package, when announced, came to $586 billion (for a headline number of 4 trillion renminbi) of new government spending in two years, on infrastructure and social welfare projects. It sounded like a New Deal. This was part of an "active" fiscal policy, while monetary policy would be "moderately active."[4] There were concerns over how much money was truly new, but markets' relief was palpable. The Shanghai Composite rose 7.3 percent the day after the announcement and never looked back. And commodities, once more, lurched on news from China. Copper rose 10 percent in a day.

There is a final reason that emerging markets bounced; unlike the United States and Western Europe, they had learned the lessons from the crises of the 1980s and 1990s. When the KIKO options debacle briefly threatened a new crisis, they showed they were not as vulnerable to the flows of international capital as they used to be. "Markets behaved the way they always do, which is that they misbehaved. They reached the ledge," said Antoine van Agtmael, who had invented emerging markets as an asset class a quarter of a century earlier. "And then people said: 'This is ridiculous.'"[5]

Agtmael used a medical analogy: "Pandemics are dangerous when the immune system is poor. But pandemics are mitigated if the immune system is good. Basically the emerging markets had better immune systems than most people thought." In other words, they had foreign exchange reserves, their consumers did not have much debt, and their banks were better regulated than before.

Not only China had stockpiled foreign reserves. Russia spent $200 billion in an (unsuccessful) attempt to defend the ruble. South Korea was sitting on $240 billion—far more than the $22 billion with which it had entered its crisis in 1997. And emerging markets were relatively cheap while government cash was available to help buy them. By the end of November 2009, $72.5 billion had flowed into emerging market funds for the year, far exceeding the previous record of $54 billion for the bubble year of 2007. That drove an epic rally. A year after hitting bottom, the emerging markets index had more than doubled, with the BRICs up 145 percent. The strongest stock market in the world over that time, gaining 195 percent, was Peru. This showed a return to self-reinforcing logic. Peru's fortune was almost entirely a function of China and its appetite for commodities like copper. And at the heart of this logic lay a recovery in China that seemed self-contradictory.[6]

China's imports of metals were so prodigious that it was hard to see how they could possibly be used. Its copper imports doubled in the first nine months of the year alone, causing the global copper price to double with it. Much of this appeared to be stockpiling, or speculation,[7] but the buying drove revivals for Peru, a big metals exporter, and other commodity-exporting countries.

The speed of the recovery, and the rapacity of China's appetite, soon generated concern. In November 2008, China had announced a "moderately active" monetary policy. What ensued could more accurately be described as "hyperactive." Aggregate new lending in the first half of 2009 ran at almost triple its level in the first half of the year before—an almost unfathomably swift expansion, which the Chinese authorities soon tried to rein in. How could such a swift boom in lending not lead to a credit bubble? Unsurprisingly, China's stock market went into a downturn, echoed elsewhere around the world, as China attempted to rein in its banks in early 2010.

China's currency adds a dangerous extra element to the mix. During the previous emerging markets bubble, which burst in the summer of 2008, the Chinese currency rose by 20 percent against the dollar in three years—and so Chinese exporters steadily became less competitive. During the rally of 2009, China's currency stayed pegged to the dollar, so outflows from dollars into countries like Brazil forced up the local currency against both the dollar and the renminbi. The effect was to make both the United States *and* China more competitive.

That provoked a political reaction, which can only intensify if the renminbi continues to get cheaper. Brazil attempted to curb the inflows in 2008 by imposing a tax on incoming investments in either

Brazilian stocks or bonds—a dramatic sign that the foreign cash was now unwelcome. Similarly, Taiwan put limits on holdings of foreigners of Taiwanese bank accounts. So did Indonesia.

Emerging markets themselves passed a critical test in 2008. With only some technical assistance from the Fed, they were strong enough to resist a crisis. This was deeply encouraging. But the investor behavior that followed it was not. If the emerging markets had matured, the investors putting money into them, it became ever more obvious, had not. That is cause for grave concern.

In Summary

- China's stimulus plan ended the debacle for emerging markets in 2008.
- Emerging market institutions are far stronger than in the 1980s and 1990s.
- The critical question is whether China's recovery is sustainable.

Chapter 26

Banks Bounce

> *"After a crash has occurred, it is important to wait long enough for the insolvent firms to fail, but not so long as to let the crisis spread to the solvent firms that need liquidity— 'delaying the death of the strong swimmers.'"*
>
> Charles P. Kindleberger[1]

World markets only recovered once investors grew confident that no more big banks would fail or be nationalized. That started a "positive feedback" loop, as confidence made financing easier to obtain in many markets. Governments won that confidence by treating banks with exceptional generosity.

The news that revived world markets came in an internal memo. From October 2008 to March 2009, Citigroup had needed four infusions from the U.S. government to stay afloat. Its share price dipped below $1, making nationalization seem inevitable. Vikram Pandit, Citi's CEO, wanted to reassure his 300,000 employees, so he told them that "we were profitable through the first two months of 2009 and are having our best quarter-to-date performance since the third quarter of 2007." He also said that deposits were "relatively sound," suggesting that there was no bank run to match the travails of the UK's Northern Rock.[2]

This was enough to spur what was arguably the most impressive rally ever seen in the U.S. stock market. That day alone, Citi's share price rose almost 40 percent, while the S&P grew 6.5 percent.[3] Just as Meredith Whitney had marked the top on Halloween 2007, more news from Citi marked the bottom 16 months later.

It had such an effect for two reasons. First, as in any down market, fear swamped greed. As Citi became a penny stock, the S&P 500 touched the ominous number of 666, erasing all of its gains since August 1996. Surveys of investors suggested confidence had never been lower. The weekly survey of the American Association of Individual Investors found 70 percent of its respondents feeling bearish—the highest on record and more pessimistic even than in the desperate weeks after the Lehman collapse. In such conditions sometimes a minor news item, such as Pandit's internal memo about unaudited figures, can turn confidence around.

Second, central banks had surgically removed the fear from the markets on which banks depend. Government cash had brought investors back into the frozen markets for commercial paper, mortgages, and corporate credit. That created cheaper financing and helped banks. For shareholders, there remained the risk that nationalization would wipe them out, but Pandit's memo reassured them on that score. That allowed money to return to equities as well.

In sum, although obscured in an alphabet soup of acronyms, the government's clear message was that no bank would be allowed to fail. Once that message was received, markets entered a positive feedback loop. Just as George Soros might predict, confidence in one market alters the reality of other markets for the better and allows them to recover. Once the central banks had convinced a few key traders that they were serious, correlation once more became a force for gains.

The U.S. government's bailout package unrolled bit by bit in the days after the correlated crash of October 2008. The Federal Reserve bought commercial paper directly, in effect putting it in the business of lending to companies that were not banks, which was a huge extension of its remit. This signaled that it was safe to buy commercial paper once more, so banks could once more borrow in the commercial paper market.

Britain's premier Gordon Brown announced a £400 billion bailout for British banks—almost as much as the $700 billion that Congress voted for the TARP, for a country less than one-fifth of the size of the United States. The government bought stakes in troubled banks, a form of nationalization, but the market liked the move. That prompted the U.S. Treasury, still controlled by Hank Paulson under President Bush, to do the same.

Paulson bought direct stakes in big banks, whether they wanted the money or not. This money raised banks' capital so that they could afford to take more losses. He followed up with targeted rescues for big banks that got into trouble, including Citigroup, which took an extra $20 billion in capital from the government, along with guarantees for a stunning $300 billion of its most problematic debt-backed securities,[4] and Bank of America, which also received $20 billion, along with guarantees of $118 billion of debt.[5] The two behemoth banks created in the Holy Week mergers of 1998 were, indeed, too big to fail—and this was a relief for the markets.

Next, there was the Term Asset-Backed Securities Loan Facility (TALF), in which the Fed offered to lend up to $200 billion to holders of student loans, auto loans, credit card loans, and small business loans—all forms of credit that were not yet deep in trouble, but gave reason to fear that the panic would soon spread. The TALF erected a firewall to stop the problem spreading to new areas.

The Fed also said that it would spend up to $600 billion buying mortgage bonds issued or guaranteed by the big agencies such as Fannie Mae and Freddie Mac. This let banks sell the more "toxic" securities on their balance sheet. It also drove up their price and persuaded some speculators to try buying them at cheap prices in the hope of later selling them to the government. The move essentially brought life back to the mortgage market.

In March came quantitative easing, the jargon for a central bank buying government bonds to push prices up and yields down—a form of printing money. Central banks hate doing this, so this was a clear sign to the markets that the Fed would stop at nothing to keep the banks from collapsing.

The Obama administration and new Treasury secretary Timothy Geithner even announced a Public-Private Investment Program (PPIP), which came close to a bribe to buy toxic assets. Banks would be invited to put up bundles of toxic debt for auction, and fund managers approved by the government would then bid for them. The money they put forward could be multiplied up to 12 times by cheap loans offered by the government—a move that directly mimicked the extreme leverage that had helped exactly these assets get overvalued in the first place. This suggested total desperation to get these markets moving. The more the assets proved to be worth, the more the exercise would cost taxpayers (because they would pay a higher price for the assets), while the fund managers, if they made a killing, would keep their leveraged profits.

In April 2009, the United States even allowed banks to fudge their accounts. Under "fair value" accounting, banks had to value their assets at the price which they could fetch in the market. They complained that in the event of a panic, they had to mark down to irrationally cheap values, even to the point of rendering themselves insolvent. The new rules, rushed through by the main U.S. accounting standards body amid complaints of political pressure from big investor groups, gave banks a little more flexibility. Rather than see the value of their assets plummet with the market, they now had some leeway to assume a higher price.

All of these measures sound like desperation. They were. But their effect on markets is best understood using game theory. Politicians were daring investors to take risks. There was no money to be made by making secure investments, because interest rates were zero. Bond yields were not going to rise because the Fed and the government would not let them. The government was not going to allow another Lehman debacle either. Moral hazard was back—if a big bank took one risk too many, they would be rescued. That made risk-taking irresistible.

Now, consider the games that individual fund managers play against each other. Staying in cash paid them nothing. Their peers, against whom they were judged, made big profits as markets recovered. Therefore, the pressure to start buying riskier assets was overwhelming, even for those who believed the government's desperation tactics would end with another crash. The herding instinct was made stronger by the effects of confidence returning to different markets. Activity returned to commercial paper markets, and then to mortgages and good-quality credit. That relieved pressure on banks (even as the economy was in freefall), so investors started buying stock.

Having launched on this strategy, governments then had to play for time, to ensure no further panic before confidence in markets could take hold. In the United States, the Obama administration did this by taking months carrying out stress tests—computer simulations to see how big banks would fare in a severe economic downturns. Many complained that they were barely even "stress" tests, as the scenarios they tested were far from the worst imaginable, but the wait for the results—which were leaked in advance—helped to take heat out of the situation.

When the stress test results appeared, they showed that ten big banks must raise an extra $75 billion in capital.[6] Months earlier, this would have been impossible, but with markets riding higher on hopes of a China-centric global recovery, banks found buyers quickly, underscoring the new-found confidence.

The strategy of playing for time had worked, at least so far. It was not indefensible—the longer that banks could continue trading with access to historically cheap credit, the longer they could accumulate profits. Those profits could be added on to their capital, steadily making them more solvent. Investors, knowing this, lined up to offer them more money to wager.

Banks (and money markets) rest on confidence. This confidence in itself reduced the toxicity of the most impaired assets, by raising their prices, and made financing easier for everyone to come by. By the end of 2009, the more successful banks were making big profits and thereby making themselves very unpopular.

But there was still ample reason to worry about the health of banks. Banks that were not too big to fail, tended to fail. In 2009, 140 U.S. banks failed, the most since deposit insurance was introduced in the 1930s.[7] Rising unemployment—which reached 10 percent in 2009—tends to bring higher defaults in its wake, much commercial real estate appeared to be overvalued, and many of the most ill-advised subprime mortgages were due to be reset to new interest rates. Any of these factors might yet overwhelm the buoyant animal spirits of the banking system—just as subprime losses had forced the credit bubble to burst in 2007.

But the calculated gamble that markets could continue their virtuous circle until the banks had dealt with the overhang of bad debt on their books carried on working for many months. In the 1930s, the greatest fear was fear itself; in the age of Barack Obama, the greatest hope for the banking system was hope itself.

In Summary

- Markets' recovery rested on recovery by the banks, which in turn rested on unprecedented and costly government attempts to bolster confidence.

- This policy avoided the bank nationalizations that had been anticipated. The critical question for 2010 and after is whether confidence can be sustained once the emergency measures end.

- If not, banks are reliant on the moral hazard created by government guarantees—and nationalization might be preferable.

Chapter 27

A New Bubble?

> *"Without due recognition of crowd-thinking (which often seems crowd-madness) our theories of economics leave much to be desired. It is a force wholly impalpable—perhaps little amenable to analysis and less to guidance—and yet, knowledge of it is necessary to right judgments on passing events."*
>
> Bernard Baruch, writing in 1934[1]

The 2009 rally was the most impressive in a century, but the signs of perverse synchronization were alarming—forex, equity, credit, and commodity markets moved in alignment, forcing some countries to try to push their currencies down, and leading to record gold prices. Many feared an incipient bubble.

The global stock market rally that started in March 2009 was the most impressive in more than a century. At its nadir, the S&P 500 hit the ominous level of 666, no higher than it had been in August 1996. From there, it gained 63.5 percent, getting back to 1120, and regaining in eight months exactly half its losses of the previous sixteen months. A "relief rally" is to be expected after a big sell-off, but after nine months, this rally was still greater than the rallies after the great bear markets of 1932, 1974, and 1982.

There was fuel for a rally because the global economy was recovering after its post-Lehman seizure and profits were stronger than expected, in large part because the downturn made it easier to cut costs by firing workers. Vocabulary shifted subtly. Pundits started talking about the "Great Panic" rather than the "Great Crash"—implying that the horrors of October 2008 were merely the result of a panic, rather than a reaction to fundamentals. If this were true, the market could indeed rebound as quickly as it had fallen, once investors got over their overwrought fears.

But it appears that the rally rested on exactly the same pathologies of herding behavior, moral hazard, and a simplistic faith in models, combined with synchronized and self-reinforcing trading, that created the super-bubble in the first place. And investors got over their panic only after truly extraordinary interventions by the U.S. and Chinese governments that must, at some point, be paid for. Rather than dismissing the entire correlated crash as a Great Panic, a more alarming and perhaps more persuasive interpretation is that the super-bubble never fully deflated before the behavior that inflated it the first time began to inflate it again.

History's great bull markets start when prices are irrationally cheap. Despite the fall that preceded it, it is hard to say that this was true in March 2009. Surveys of investors did show exceptional pessimism in March 2009, thanks to worries about a populist backlash against the bail-outs, or a choking off of free trade, and the arrival of the untried President Obama.

But stocks were much cheaper, and the economy in even greater trouble, before history's other great rallies began. A reliable long-term measure is the cyclically adjusted price/earnings ratio, first conceived by Ben Graham and more recently championed by Robert Shiller of Yale University. This metric compares share prices to average earnings over the previous ten years, and correctly identifies 1929 and 2000 as the two historical points when the U.S. stock market was most crazily overvalued. It also spots market lows. The cyclically adjusted price/earnings ratio fell to 5.5 before markets recovered in 1932, and almost fell to 7 before the rally of 1982 (see Figure 27.1).[2]

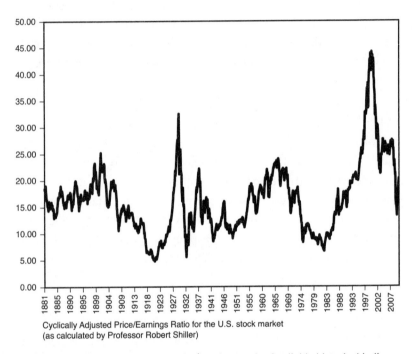

Cyclically Adjusted Price/Earnings Ratio for the U.S. stock market
(as calculated by Professor Robert Shiller)

Figure 27.1 *Cyclically adjusted price/earnings ratio: A reliable historical indicator says stocks are expensive.*

In 2009, the cyclically adjusted price/earnings ratio never fell below 13, suggesting stocks needed to be far cheaper before they presented a truly compelling buying opportunity; and by the end of the year it was back above 20, well above the historic average and almost identical to its level on the eve of the Lehman debacle (although, it must be stressed, still well below the levels that marked previous bubbles). That in turn implies that the desperate measures to save the banking system lifted the stock market before speculative excess had been squeezed out. And that is easy to believe. It is, after all, exactly what happened in 2003, when cheap money from the Fed arrested the decline in stocks and ignited the credit bubble, before the effects of the dot-com bubble had been squeezed from the system. As the chart shows, the 2003 rebound came, otherwise incomprehensibly, when stocks were still historically expensive.

Next, as Figure 27.2 shows, the rise in stocks correlated almost perfectly with the decline in the dollar, precisely repeating the perverse pattern of the super-bubble years. As investors regained their appetite for risk, so they took their money out of the United States. The correlation weakened slightly but remained intact, with the dollar rising as stocks fell early in 2010. The parallels with Japan's crash of 1990 are eerie. It kept its banks alive while cutting interest rates to zero, and then the world used its currency to borrow cheap. In 2009, exactly the same thing happened to the dollar. The money flowing out of the United States was executing a kind of dollar carry trade, as investors looked for higher yields elsewhere.

Then there is the issue of correlation. According to MSCI, the correlation of the BRICs and the emerging markets with the developed world reached an all-time high in the summer of 2009. By then, the rolling annual correlation between them was above 0.8—so that a move in one was by far the strongest explanation for a move in the other.[3]

In late 2009, correlations between the stock market and the carry trade were also stronger than at any point in 2007 or 2008—with the significant difference that the weak currency traders borrowed was the dollar, not the Japanese yen. The dollar and U.S. stocks were tightly linked (refer to Figure 27.2). So, still, were the yen carry trade and the oil market (see Figure 27.3). Calculations by Jamie Lee of pi Economics show that moves in the S&P 500 were by now sufficient to explain 60 percent of moves in the exchange rate of the Australian dollar against the U.S. dollar. For commodity-backed carry trade currencies as a whole, the S&P explained about half their movements. And the link between the yen and the S&P was stronger than it had been in the weeks after the Shanghai Surprise almost three years earlier, when markets first lapsed into crisis.

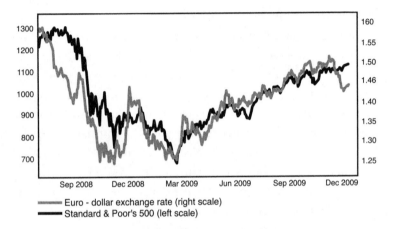

Euro - dollar exchange rate (right scale)
Standard & Poor's 500 (left scale)

Figure 27.2 *U.S. stocks only gain as the dollar loses.*

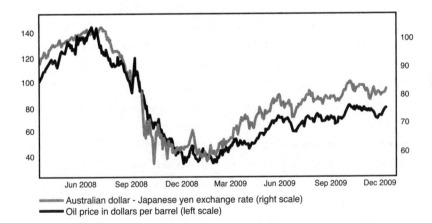

Australian dollar - Japanese yen exchange rate (right scale)
Oil price in dollars per barrel (left scale)

Figure 27.3 *Oil and the carry trade: still locked together*

Such strong correlations may merely be the result of the correlated crash that preceded them. If all these markets became undervalued together in a panic, then they might well be linked with each other on the way back up. But the pattern of the synchronicity between world markets makes this very hard to believe. Not only did markets take their cues from the falling dollar, but they took fresh orders almost every minute. Over a six-week period, the exchange rates of the dollar against the euro, the Australian dollar, and the price of gold all had a correlation of more than 0.5 with the U.S. stock market, *every minute*. Even in weeks when neither had a clear overall trend, they moved in the same direction as each other almost three times as often as they moved in opposite directions.

As the historical relationship between these markets is minimal, this suggested that all of them were priced inefficiently—bad news when the world economy was fighting to find equilibrium after a free fall. The relationship is so tight that it may be caused by computer-driven funds that have tracked the relationship in the past and are trading on the assumption that it will continue. If a computer-driven fund sees a gain in the S&P, it automatically buys the Australian dollar, for example.

Another explanation for 2009's resurgence is that markets entered a "rational bubble."[4] On this view, the banks' recovery relied on co-opting, or abusing, the U.S. government's credit rating. In 2009, the United States stood as the ultimate guarantor of U.S. bank debt and issued much more debt to stimulate its economy. It could do this because its credit is rated higher than any other nation on the planet. To use an uncomfortable analogy, it is in the same position as the giant insurer AIG before the crash. AIG's AAA rating, although undeserved, allowed many securities to trade for more than they were worth. Its downgrade was a moment of truth for the market.

Much the same would happen, although with no guarantor of last resort to step in, if the market were to lose its confidence in the

United States and its AAA credit rating. But the U.S. government has tax-raising powers, and the likelihood of default remains remote. Therefore in the medium-term, fund managers who do not want to look stupid and lose assets should rationally stay invested in the market, as the rally will continue until the bond market loses faith in the U.S. government's creditworthiness and forces up interest rates. This is in line with history, as the U.S. bond market allowed the great bull market to start in 1982, when yields fell post-Volcker and later triggered the collapse of 2007 when yields rose.

Fund managers who wanted to keep their jobs had even stronger reasons to buy. Once the market turned, they desperately needed to be a part of the action to avoid embarrassment. The weight of money programmed to follow the herd also increased. Index funds and exchange-traded funds gained ground. By the end of 2009, ETFs of both commodities and stocks, on both sides of the Atlantic, had more assets than at their peak before the crisis. An ever larger chunk of the market automatically chased prices higher. Hence it may indeed be "rational" for investors to buy into the great rally of 2009—even if this involves inflating an incipient bubble.

A final concern is that traders were playing chicken with the Fed once more and betting that central banks would not dare exit their cheap money policies. After the disastrous United States attempt to beat moral hazard by letting Lehman Brothers go bankrupt, the market assumed that the government would not follow through on any threat to raise rates.

This was a key difference from the bear market lows of 1932 and 1982.[5] On these occasions, financial pain had squeezed moral hazard out of the system. Investors were humbled. In 2009, despite the disasters of 2007 and 2008, politicians made a conscious decision to reignite risk-taking, to jump-start the market. The alternative of revisiting the worst depths of 1932 seemed too dangerous given the populist sentiment around the world, with attacks on the homes of bankers and riots in the streets. But the option they chose is also a dangerous game. The more commodity prices rise and the dollar weakens, the greater the risk of inflation, and hence the greater the incentive for the Fed to swerve and raise rates to choke it off. Bastille Day of 2008, when the oil price collapsed, warns what could happen.

The word "bubble" can itself be devalued. By the end of 2009, stocks were still far below their highs, and were nowhere near as overvalued as they were before previous crashes. There was still time to stave off a new bubble. But it was remarkable that stocks were more expensive than the historical norm with the financial system still on life support. All of the perverse incentives and instabilities that had marked the investment industry as it grew up over the preceding half century remained embedded in global markets' DNA. The most absurd and debased financial instruments of the subprime debacle were gone and were never to return, but the incentives that had allowed synthetic collateralized debt obligations and the like to flourish remained in place. The danger is that another, more severe financial dislocation will be needed finally to purge the markets of these distortions.

In Summary

- The forces driving the great 2009 rally were moral hazard and the herding mentality of the modern investment industry.

- Tight correlations suggest markets were priced inefficiently, even if prices remained below bubble territory.

- Reform is needed to change incentives on fund managers and reduce moral hazard before new super-bubbles form.

2010 and After

> *"It is the long-term investor, he who most promotes the public interest, who will in practice come in for most criticism, wherever investment funds are managed by committees or boards or banks. For it is in the essence of his behaviour that he should be eccentric, unconventional and rash in the eyes of average opinion.... Worldly wisdom teaches that it is better for reputation to fail conventionally than to succeed unconventionally."*
>
> John Maynard Keynes in *The General Theory*

The condition is easily diagnosed. Over the last half century, the rise of the investment industry has created overwhelming incentives for investors to follow one another into risks they often do not understand. As a result, world markets are hopelessly synchronized. This obstructs rational pricing and, in a capitalist world that relies on markets to set prices, endangers our prosperity. Finding a cure, however, is more difficult.

The financial disaster of 2007–2009 has not cured any of the underlying factors that led markets to become intertwined and over-inflated. They may still not be addressed even if, as is possible, the world navigates the next few years without a second recession or a major new collapse in stocks, real estate, or other assets. If the twin planks of the recovery—China's resurgence and the ability of big U.S. banks to "muddle through" with government help—stay in place, then the prospects for a recovery are good. But the stakes are higher now. Markets turned in 2009 because the United States put its credit rating on the line by borrowing furiously while extending guarantees to many private companies and securities that were in trouble. By setting the price of money, the U.S. Treasury market drives all others, and if bond investors decide that mountainous U.S. debt will lead to inflation or to default by Uncle Sam, yields will rise. The crisis of confidence in the debt of countries like Portugal and Greece shows what could happen. And in such circumstances, the U.S. Treasury will not be able to help because it will not be able to borrow more. Thus, the next asset price crash could be profoundly worse than the last one— and this makes the need to cure the underlying conditions that lead to crashes all the more urgent.

Some fixes are easy. The absurdly complicated instruments that created the subprime bubble, like synthetic collateralized debt obligations, should of course go. But the roots of the problem lie deeper. The institutionalization of investment cannot be reversed. Most of the financial innovations that created the synchronized bubble, like index funds, or even securitized mortgages, are in any case good ideas, so finding fixes will involve hard choices.

Making this harder, solutions must deal with human nature, our tendencies to suffer swings of emotion, to move in herds, and to expect that others will rescue us from the consequences of our actions. Over the last half century, the investing industry has unwittingly intensified those tendencies. Changing this requires a cultural shift; investors must have an incentive to treat others' money as if it were their own. The following is an outline of how markets can be made more fearful, and maybe more efficient.

Moral Hazard

Previous financial crises reined in moral hazard—the encouragement to take risks that comes when investors believe they will not have to suffer losses—by inflicting grievous losses on key investors. The latest crisis was very different—it showed that the United States and other governments would spend trillions of dollars to sustain the biggest financial groups. Hence the belief that risk takers will be rescued is stronger than ever. Air must be taken out of markets that at the time of writing, in early 2010, are currently betting that the government dare not let them fail. It is still too soon to do it. But at some point, either by raising rates or by allowing a big bank to go down, government must make clear it will not be there to bail out the reckless.

A safe place to start would be the megabanks like Bank of America, which are even bigger as a result of shotgun mergers arranged during the crisis. They cannot be allowed to fail. Either these biggest banks must be regulated so tightly that they simply are not allowed to gamble, or they must be made smaller. Governments can allow the market some say if they do this by raising reserve requirements, which in practice would force banks to sell off assets. This need not involve imposing a breakup. But the growing political debate over how to regulate banks and make them smaller is not just a response to populist anger; some such move is necessary if moral hazard is ever to be addressed.

The Decline of Banks and the Rise of Markets

The rise of money markets created a new class of bank-like institutions that do not need to buy deposit insurance. This shadow banking system, including money market funds, must now be regulated as if they were banks. Reforms to solidify the repo market, which denied banks their short-term funding when it seized up, are vital. And regulators need to overhaul the rules that inadvertently spurred banks to pile into mortgage-backed securities and outsource to rating agencies like Standard & Poor's their central function as lenders—figuring out who can pay back a loan and who cannot.

What remains of the banking industry has lost its old roles and, like unemployed teenage boys, they have shown a terrible knack for getting into trouble when they are left to their own devices. Once money markets are subject to the same regulation as banks, their advantages may evaporate, enabling banks to regain their old businesses of lending. If not, the economy can possibly do without banks in their traditional form. Hedge funds drove many trends to destruction by 2007, but the much-feared disorderly collapse of a big hedge fund did not occur. Instead, it was the inherent instability of banks that brought the roof down. And so for banks, the *status quo* is not an option.

Other People's Money

Reforms to the banking system must also address the conflicts between principals and agents that arise whenever those who take on a risk are able to sell that risk to other parties. In securitization, where some principal-agent split is inevitable, loan originators must be required to hold a significant proportion of their loan portfolio or in other words to "eat their own cooking."

Investment banks that are now public might return to the partnership model. Then the money on the line would be that of the partners themselves, not shareholders. Again this might not require government intervention. Existing investment banks, who probably dislike all the attention on the bonuses they pay, could go private. Or hedge funds, which are structured as partnerships and increasingly already carry out investment banking functions, could evolve further. The trickiest principal-agent split, however, affects investment managers.

Herding

The herd mentality of the current generation of investment managers is driven by the way they are paid and ranked. Rank them against their peers and an index, and pay them by how much money they manage, and experience shows that they will hug ever closer to key benchmarks like the S&P 500. So somehow we must change the way we pay fund managers.

For hedge funds, which are not closely regulated, it is up to investors to refuse to pay fees on the skewed basis that at present encourages them to gear up to "go for broke" each year. Paying fixed annual fees, while basing any performance fees on periods much longer than one year, would make more sense.

In mutual funds, it is far too easy for mediocrities to make money in an upward market. Their fees go up merely for taking in more funds. Closet indexing must be actively discouraged, possibly by requiring "active" funds to publish their "active share" (the amount their portfolio deviates from the index). Closet indexing might also be rendered less harmful if mainstream index funds moved toward fundamental indexing, weighting their portfolios according to fundamentals such as profits, rather than their market price. This forces them, and anyone mimicking them, to sell stocks as they become overvalued. Paying managers a fixed fee would no longer reward them merely for accumulating assets, and so funds would be less likely to grow too big. Rewards above a fixed fee should only be for genuinely excellent performance. This brings up the greatest problem; how to determine that performance? In professions, performance-related pay relies on benchmarks, but we now know that benchmarking portfolio managers against their peers, or against a market index, just encourages them to herd together.

The solution may lie in the growing effort to understand and measure investing skill. It rests in mental discipline and the ability to resist the temptations of greed, panic, and mental shortcuts. By looking at how fund managers perform day by day and trade by trade, psychologists are beginning to identify the truly talented, and separate them from those who fall into mental traps and whose performance might look perfectly acceptable for long periods. This effort should continue. Skillful investors can, after all, profit while keeping the market more efficient at the same time.

The greatest power rests with those who make big asset allocation decisions—primarily brokers and pension fund consultants. They should follow what is called a "barbell"—either their investments are passive, with minimal costs, or they are given to active managers on the basis of their skill, who are paid according to that skill. There is no room for anything in between.

Another needed reform would change the design of investment products so as to deliver everyone from temptation. Rather than give savers a range of choices, give them a well-tailored default option, covering a sensible distribution across the main asset classes, with both passive and active management. To maintain investors' confidence, it may make sense to declare guaranteed gains along the way, much as the old Victorian model of paternalistic pensions did. Libertarians might dislike this, but the default option should not be compulsory. You can choose something else if you wish. The key is that the default should be a good one and not overloaded by fees.

The industry is already moving in this direction.[1] This should restore investors' confidence, avert the risk that "irrational exuberance" might again drive markets, and limit the worries for all managers about their success in accumulating assets. Instead, and quite healthily, they would merely have to worry about performing skillfully enough to earn a bonus.

Safety in Numbers

The old theory of diversification prompted overconfidence and created the rush into "uncorrelated" assets that then became linked. Core assumptions, like stable correlations over time, random returns, and emphasis on allocation by asset classes, have failed and must go. We need a new theory. Academics are already on the case.

Paul Woolley of the London School of Economics believes efficient markets might be salvaged if we can find a way to model the distorting effects of institutions on incentives. Andrew Lo, of the Massachusetts Institute of Technology, suggests markets are complex adaptive systems that can be modeled using Darwinian biology—which implies we are living in an era when a meteor has just hit the earth and we await the successors to the dinosaurs. But any new model must not aspire to the same precision as the old; finance and economics are contingent on human decision making and not the laws of nature. Abandon the attempt to predict markets with precision, and we might avert a return to the overconfidence such models created in the past.

As for diversification, those who allocate assets must stop thinking in terms of asset classes and the historic correlations between them. The search for new "uncorrelated" asset classes helped lead to disaster. Instead, they must look at the risks those assets bear and leave a margin for error—meaning more in "conservative" assets, and less potential "upside," than they would like. Again, thankfully, such ideas are already bubbling through the investment industry.

All of these ideas involve putting limits on the wealth that markets can create, which is akin to the trade-off the world made after the Depression. Many would now be happy to make that trade-off again, even though, with the capitalist world aging, the growth rate we can expect in the next few decades may well be significantly lower than in the second half of the twentieth century.

The cycle of greed and fear is hard-wired into human nature. But this list of changes might just end the cycle of synchronized bubbles, avert another even more disastrous crash within the next few years, and move back to the norm where we can go two generations without a new bubble. Further, markets should distribute capital much more efficiently. They might even shower capital on technologies and innovations that can improve our well being, rather than sending resources and talents to an artificially bloated financial services industry.

Markets have risen to take a far greater role in our lives. If they can be disentangled and unsynchronized, they will work better for everyone.

Notes

Chapter 1

[1]See J.K. Galbraith, *The Great Crash 1929* (Boston: Penguin, 1954).

[2]Charles P. Kindleberger and Robert Aliber, *Manias, Panics and Crashes*, 5th ed. (New York:Wiley, 2005). This is the definitive history of asset bubbles.

Chapter 2

[1]See John Authers, "Victim of Its Own Success," *Financial Times*, January 22, 1997, Section (if any), Edition; and John Authers, "Mutuals Manage to Miss the Track," *Financial Times*, January 11, 1997.

[2]See John Authers and Elizabeth Wine, "Jeffrey Vinik to leave fund management,"by *Financial Times*, October 27, 2000. He made annual returns of 53 percent per year for four years and closed before the crash of 2000 could dent his returns.

[3]Jim Melcher, conversation with the author, December 1, 2009. Melcher went on to make returns of more than 200 per cent in 2007, after successfully betting on the end of the credit bubble.

[4]In 2007, shortly before his death at the age of 60, Tony Dye wrote to the *Financial Times* saying that the world financial system needed a "clean-out of Augean stable proportions"—a judgment that also proved correct.

Chapter 3

[1]Quoted from John C. Bogle, *Common Sense on Mutual Funds*, 10th Anniversary Edition, (Hoboken, NJ: Wiley, 2009), 155.

[2]See Burton Malkiel, *A Random Walk Down Wall Street*, (New York: Norton, 2007),

[3]Figures are from *Common Sense on Mutual Funds*.

[4]See Peter Bernstein, *Capital Ideas Evolving*, (Somerset, NJ: Wiley, 2005).

[5]*Common Sense on Mutual Funds*, 335.

[6]See Benoit Mandelbrot and Richard L. Hudson, *The (Mis)Behavior of Markets—A Fractal View of Financial Turbulence*, (New York: Basic Books, 2004), 94.

[7]See Justin Fox, *The Myth of Rational Markets*, (New York: Collins Business, 2009) for a definitive study of the academic politics behind the break-throughs in rational markets.

[8]Ibid., 105.

[9]See Antte Petajisto, *Magellan's Problem: Closet Indexing*, November 15, 2005, http://www.petajisto.net/media/magellan_oped.pdf.

[10]See Jason Zweig, "Inside the world's largest fund," *Money Magazine*, April 15, 2002.

[11]See K.J. Martijn Cremers and Antte Petajisto, "How Active is Your Fund Manager? A New Measure That Predicts Performance," March 31, 2009, http://papers.ssrn.com/sol3/papers.cfm?abstract_id=891719.

Chapter 4

[1]Taken from The Reserve Fund's Annual Report to investors, July 2008—written a few weeks before the fund sustained a loss on Lehman bonds and closed itself to investors, triggering the world's worst financial panic in at least a century.

[2]Figures are drawn from William Greider, *Secrets of the Temple—How the Federal Reserve Runs the Country*, (New York: Simon and Schuster, 1987).

[3]Paul Volcker speaking at the Chicago Mercantile Exchange's Global Financial Leadership Conference (Naples, Florida, November 2, 2009).

[4]Paul Schott Stephens, "Of Black Swans and Money Funds" (speaking at the Investment Company Institute, New York City, October 6, 2008).

Chapter 5

[1]See Greider, *Secrets of the Temple—How the Federal Reserve Runs the Country*, 337.

[2]See Charles R. Morris, *The Sages—Warren Buffett, George Soros, Paul Volcker and the Maelstrom of Markets*, (New York: Public Affairs, 2009), 126.

[3]See James Grant, *Mr. Market Miscalculates—The Bubble Years and Beyond*, (Edinburg, Virginia: Axios, 2008), xvii.

[4]See Bureau of Labor and Statistics, "Databases, Tables & Calculators by Subject," http://data.bls.gov.

Chapter 6

[1]See Federal Deposit Insurance Corporation's Division of Research and Statistics, "History of the Eighties—Lessons for the Future Volume 1, An Examination of the Banking Crisis of the 1980s and Early 1990s," http://www.fdic.gov/bank/historical/history/191_210.pdf. Chapter 5 covers the LDCs crisis.

[2]Quoted in Moira Johnston, *The tumultuous history of the Bank of America*, (Frederick, Maryland: Beard Books, 2000), 181.

[3]López Portillo lived until 2004. He was never forgiven, and whenever he entered a restaurant, Mexicans would bark derisively. Short of funds late in life, he even resorted to giving his name to a new brand of tequila.

[4]Antoine van Agtmael, conversation with the author, September 2009.

[5]Quoted from Antoine van Agtmael, *The Emerging Markets Century—How a New Breed of World-Class Companies is Overtaking the World*, (New York: Free Press, 2007), 5.

[6]Figures provided by Peter Veto of MSCI Barra.

Chapter 7

[1]Michael Lewis, *Liar's Poker: Rising Through the Wreckage on Wall Street*, (New York: Penguin, 1990).

[2]See "Trends and Cycles in Corporate Bond Financing" by W. Braddock Hickman, National Bureau of Economic Research, 1952.

[3]See Bryan Burrough and John Helyar, *Barbarians at the Gate*, (New York: Random Century, 1990).

[4]Figures cited in James B. Stewart, *Den of Thieves*, (Riverside, NJ: Simon & Schuster, 1991), 503–504.

Chapter 8

[1]These figures are based on Datastream equity indices.

[2]See Kindleberger and Aliber, *Manias, Panics and Crashes*, x.

[3]See Gabriele Galati and Michael Melvin, "Why has FX trading surged? Explaining the 2004 triennial survey," *BIS Quarterly Review*, December 2004.

[4]See Christopher Condon and Peter Garnham, "Swiss franc wins foreign favour in funding asset purchases," *Financial Times*, March 22, 2007.

Chapter 9

[1]See Anatole Kaletsky, "How Mr Soros made a billion by betting against the pound," *The Times* of London, October 26, 1992.

[2]See David O. Beim and Charles Calomiris, *Emerging Financial Markets*, (New York: McGraw Hill, 2001).

[3]See "Triennial Central Bank Survey," *Bank of International Settlements*, http://www.bis.org/publ/rpfxf07t.htm.

Chapter 10

[1]See Steve Thompson, "Greenspan Speech Triggers Big Market Slide," *Financial Times*, December 7, 1996.

[2]See John Authers and Emiko Terazono, "Sales of mutual funds hit record—Concerns grow that bull market may have given retail investors unrealistic expectations," *Financial Times*, April 14,1998.

[3]Figures come from Kindleberger and Aliber, *Manias, Panics and Crashes* 156–7.

[4]See Beim and Calomiris, *Emerging Financial Markets*.

[5]See John Authers, "Growling at the bears—Everyman in the News," *Financial Times*, October 22, 1997.

Chapter 11

[1]See John Authers and Richard Wolffe, *The Victim's Fortune—Inside the Epic Battle Over the Debts of the Holocaust*, (New York: Harper Collins, 2002).

[2]See David O. Beim, "Europe and the Financial Crisis," Columbia Business School, March 17, 2009, http://www1.gsb.columbia.edu/mygsb/faculty/research/pubfiles/3324/Europe%20and%20the%20Financial%20Crisis%2Epdf.

[3]See Tracy Corrigan, "Goldman chief to net $206m from offering," *Financial Times*, April 13, 1999.

[4]Details of Basel rules, and the debate over overhauling them, are updated at www.bis.org.

[5]See John Authers, "Regulation plea over bank 'mega-mergers,'" *Financial Times*, April 29, 1998.

Chapter 12

[1]The figure comes from the definitive and highly entertaining account of the LTCM disaster: Roger Lowenstein, *When Genius Failed—The Rise and Fall of Long-Term Capital Management*, (Maryland: Random House, 2000), 219.

[2]Ibid.

[3]Ibid, 188.

[4]See John Authers, "Nothing to fear save uncertainty," *Financial Times*, October 10, 1998.

Chapter 13

[1]Richard Tomkins, "The virtual investment. Billions Were Poured Into Internet-Related Companies," *Financial Times*, December 5, 2000.

[2]All the hedge fund statistics in this chapter are drawn from the Hedge Fund Research Media Reference Guide for October 2009, available from www.hedgefundresearch.com.

Chapter 14

[1]See Goldman Sachs Economics Group, *The World and the BRICs Dream*, (New York: 2006). It includes five years of subsequent research on the BRICs.

[2]See Jack Bogle, *The Little Book of Common-Sense Investing*, (Somerset, NJ: Wiley, 2007).

³This figure goes up to when the BRICs peaked, but the returns that this investor would have made by holding on until November 2009, a year after the crash, were still a barely credible 512 percent. Over this time, the BRICs' share of the world's total market value rose six-fold.

⁴See "Emerging Markets: Latent Demand," note by Global Wealth Allocation of London, November 13, 2009.

Chapter 15

¹Gary. B Gorton, and K. Geert Rouwenhorst, "Facts and Fantasies about Commodity Futures," Yale ICF Working Paper No. 04-20, February 28, 2005, http://ssrn.com/abstract=560042.

²See "Strategic Asset Allocation and Commodities," March 27, 2006, http://www.pimco.com/LeftNav/Viewpoints/2006/Ibbotson+Commodity+Study.htm.

³See Daniel Whitten and Alan Bjerga, "Lieberman May Seek New Rules on Commodity Speculators," *Bloomberg*, May 20, 2008.

⁴Gary Gorton, conversation with the author, Decmber 4, 2009.

⁵See Chris Watling, monthly bulletin, Longview Economics, November 2007.

⁶This figure comes from Rob Carnell of ING Economics.

⁷See "Emerging Markets: Latent Demand," note issued by Global Wealth Allocation, November 13, 2009.

Chapter 16

¹See Gillian Tett, *Fool's Gold: How Unrestrained Greed Corrupted a Dream, Shattered Global Markets and Unleashed a Catastrophe*, (New York: Little, Brown, 2009), for the definitive account of how bankers developed credit derivative technology.

[2]Figures are available online at www.isda.org.

[3]Quoted in Richard Beales, "Industry on smooth learning curve with Corrigan report," *Financial Times*, September 24, 2006.

Chapter 17

[1]Ben Bernanke himself devoted a speech to the "Great Moderation" in 2004. It is available at http://www.federalreserve.gov/BOARDDOCS/SPEECHES/2004/20040220/default.htm.

[2]See Hyman Minsky, *John Maynard Keyes* (New York: McGraw Hill, 2008) 125.

[3]See John Authers and Anuj Gangahar, "Correlation' rather than 'contagion,'" *Financial Times*, February 28, 2007.

[4]See Michiyo Nakamoto and David Wighton, "Bullish Citigroup is 'still dancing' to the beat of the buy-out boom," *Financial Times*, July 10, 2007.

Chapter 18

[1]See Ben White and Saskia Scholtes, "Bear Stearns hedge fund on brink of failure after bad subprime bets," *Financial Times*, June 20, 2007.

[2]See Saskia Scholtes, "Bear Stearns shock waves gain new force" *Financial Times*, July 18, 2007.

[3]See Amir E. Khandaniy and Andrew W. Lo, "What Happened to the Quants in August 2007?" www.ssrn.com.

[4]See Peter Thal Larsen, "Goldman pays the price of being big," *Financial Times*, August 13, 2007.

[5]Joanna Chung, "Two ex-Bear Stearns fund chiefs cleared of misleading investors," *Financial Times*, November 11, 2009.

Chapter 19

[1]The clip of Cramer's outburst is widely available on the Internet and has been placed several times on www.youtube.com.

[2]See *Harry Potter and the Deathly Hallows* by J.K. Rowling.

[3]For a detailed account of how the repo market works, and how it failed in 2007, see Gary B. Gorton, *Slapped by the Invisible Hand—The Panic of 2007* (New York: Oxford University Press, 2010).

[4]See John Authers, "The Short View: Countrywide Crunch," *Financial Times*, August 23, 2007.

Chapter 20

[1]See Galbraith, *The Great Crash 1929*.

[2]In full disclosure, Mr. Peston and the author were colleagues for many years at the *Financial Times*.

[3]"Northern Rock gets bank bail out," BBC, September 13, 2007.

[4]Quoted in Martin Mayer, The Fed—The Inside Story of How the World's Most Powerful Financial Institution Drives the Markets, (New York: Free Press, 2001), 159.

[5]See Paul J. Davies and David Wighton, "Citi slashes SIV fund exposure," Financial Times, December 11, 2007.

[6]See Francesco Guerrera, "On Wall St: Super fund pill can't treat the SIV illness," *Financial Times*, December 7, 2007.

[7]Note that this estimate proved to be hugely understated. See Chris Bryant and Anora Mahmudova, "Citigroup leads financials to a five-year low," *Financial Times*, November 2, 2007.

[8]For a detailed account of the fall of Bear Stearns, see *Street Fighters* by Kate Kelly, or *The Sellout* by Charles Gasparino.

Chapter 21

[1]George Soros, speaking in Budapest, October 2009. Text provided to the author.

Chapter 22

[1]Quoted on the cover of Andrew Ross Sorkin, *Too Big To Fail—The inside story of how Wall Street and Washington fought to save the financial system—and themselves* (New York: Viking, 2009).

[2]See the account in *Too Big To Fail*. It suggests Lehman might have been rescued by Barclays of the United Kingdom, but for the refusal by British regulators to allow the deal, which the United States had not anticipated.

Chapter 23

[1]Art Cashin, interviewed by author at the NYSE, September 9, 2009. See video at http://www.ft.com/cms/bfba2c48-5588-11dc-b971-0000779fd2ac.html?_i_referralObject=9565051&fromSearch=n

[2]See Beim, "Europe and the Financial Crisis," *Columbia Business School*.

[3]See Financial Times reporters, "Pressure Grows on Europe to Protect Banks," *Financial Times*, October 1, 2008.

[4]See Bertrand Benoit, James Wilson and agencies, "Germany guarantees savings," *Financial Times*, October 5, 2008. Note that in Germany, bank assets came to almost three times GDP.

Chapter 24

[1]See John Authers, "Short View: Diversification," *Financial Times*, January 29, 2009.

[2]See RAFI Fundamentals newsletter, January 2009, http://www.researchaffiliates.com/ideas/pdf/Fundamentals_200901.pdf.

[3]See Elroy Dimson, Paul Marsh, and Mike Staunton, *Triumph of the Optimists: 101 Years of Global Investment Returns*, (Princeton, NJ: Princeton University Press, 2002).

[4]See Elroy Dimson, Paul Marsh, and Mike Staunton, "The Worldwide Equity Premium: A Smaller Puzzle," *London Business School*, January 2007.

[5]See *Triumph of the Optimists*.

[6]See Robert Arnott, "Bonds: Why Bother?" *Journal of Indexes*, May/June 2009, http://www.indexuniverse.com/publications/journalofindexes/joi-articles/5710-bonds-why-bother.html?Itemid=11.

Chapter 25

[1]See Randall Dodd, "Playing with Fire," *Finance & Development* (2009).

[2]See Krishna Guha, "Fed Supports Emerging Economies," *Financial Times*, October 30, 2008.

[3]See Tom Mitchell, "Slowdown Forces Rethink on Social Compact," *Financial Times*, November 10, 2008.

[4]See Geoff Dyer, "China Authorises 'Massive' Stimulus Package," *Financial Times*, November 9, 2008.

[5]Antoine van Agtmael, conversation with the author, October 6, 2009.

[6]See John Authers, "Short View: China's bubble," *Financial Times*, August 12, 2009.

[7]John Dizard "A copper kettle mania in China has boiled up for a bull market," *Financial Times*, November 14, 2009.

Chapter 26

[1]See Kindleberger, *Manias, Panics, and Crashes*, 241. Kindleberger was quoting J.H. Clapham, the historian of the Bank of England.

[2]See Francesco Guerrera, "Citi Has Strong Start to the Year," *Financial Times*, March 10, 2009.

[3]See Francesco Guerrera and Michael MacKenzie, "Citigroup Helps Lift Markets Worldwide," *Financial Times*, March 11, 2009.

[4]See Greg Farrell, Henny Sender, and Andrew Ward, "U.S. Agrees Bailout for Citigroup," *Financial Times*, November 24, 2008.

[5]See Sundeep Tucker, "Bank of America gets $138bn Lifeline," *Financial Times*, January 15, 2009.

[6]Krishna Guha, Francesco Guerrera, and Alan Rappeport, "Stress Tests Show $75bn Buffer Needed," by *Financial Times*, May 7 2009.

[7]Up-to-date statistics are available online at http://www.fdic.gov/bank/individual/failed/banklist.html.

Chapter 27

[1]Cited in Robert Menschel, *Markets, Mobs & Mayhem—A Modern Look at the Madness of Crowds*, (NewYork: Wiley, 2002).

[2]Figures are drawn from Professor Shiller's website. The data is downloadable in Excel format from http://www.econ.yale.edu/~shiller/data/ie_data.xls.

[3]Figures provided by Peter Veto of MSCI. Barra.

[4]See Crispin Odey, "It may be a bubble but it's completely rational," *Financial Times*, September 23, 2009.

[5]Russell Napier, *Anatomy of the Bear*, (Hong Kong: CLSA Press) is the definitive financial history of these bear market bottoms.

Conclusion

[1]See Richard Thaler and Cass Sunstein, *Nudge—Improving Decisions About Health, Wealth, and Happiness*, (New York: Penguin, 2008), for a clear (and very influential) exposition of how offering default options could be good public policy in practice.

Select Bibliography

These books were useful in preparing this book, and are recommended to provide much extra background.

Chapter 1

Chancellor, Edward. *Devil Take the Hindmost*. New York, Farrar, Strauss and Giroux 1999.

Galbraith, J.K. *The Great Crash 1929*. Boston: Penguin, 1954.

Kindleberger, Charles and Robert Aliber. *Manias, Panics and Crashes—A History of Financial Crises*. 5th ed. New York: Wiley, 2005.

Chapter 2

Akerlof, George A. and Robert J. Shiller. *Animal Spirits—How Human Psychology Drives the Economy, and Why It Matters for Global Capitalism*. Princeton, NJ: Princeton University Press, 2009.

Ariely, Dan. *Predictably Irrational—The Hidden Forces That Shape Our Decisions*. New York: Harper, 2008.

Mauboussin, Michael. *Think Twice—Harnessing the Power of Counterintuition*. Boston: Harvard Business Press, 2009.

Montier, James. *Behavioural Investing—A practitioner's guide to applying behavioural finance*. Somerset, NJ.: Wiley Finance, 2007.

Chapter 3

Bernstein, Peter L. *Capital Ideas Evolving*. Somerset, NJ: Wiley, 2006.

Bogle, Jack. *Common-Sense on Mutual Funds—New Imperatives for the Intelligent Investor*. Somerset, NJ: Wiley, 1999.

Bogle, John C. *The Little Book of Common-Sense Investing: The Only Way to Guarantee Your Fair Share of Stock Market Returns*. Somerset, NJ: Wiley, 2007.

Fox, Justin. *The Myth of Rational Markets—A History of Risk, Reward, and Delusion on Wall Street*. New York: Collins Business, 2009.

Malkiel, Burton G. *A Random Walk Down Wall Street: The Time-Tested Strategy for Successful Investing* New York: Norton, 2007.

Mandelbrot, Benoit and Richard L. Hudson. *The (mis)Behavior of Markets—A Fractal View of Financial Turbulence*. New York: Basic Books, 2004.

Smithers, Andrew. *Wall Street Revalued: Imperfect Markets and Inept Central Bankers*. Somerset, NJ: Wiley, 2009.

Chapter 4

Chernow, Ron. *The Death of the Banker—The Decline and Fall of the Great Financial Dynasties and the Triumph of the Small Investor*. New York: Random House, 1997.

Chapter 5

Grant, James. *Mr. Market Miscalculates—The Bubble Years and Beyond*. Edinburg, Virginia: Axios, 2008.

Greider, William. *Secrets of the Temple*. New York: Simon & Schuster, 1991.

Morris, Charles R. *The Sages—Warren Buffett, George Soros, Paul Volcker and the Maelstrom of Markets*. New York: Public Affairs, 2009.

Chapter 6

Beim, David O. and Charles W. Calomiris. *Emerging Financial Markets*. New York: McGraw Hill, 2001.

Van Agtmael, Antoine. *The Emerging Markets Century—How a New Breed of World-Class Companies Is Overtaking the World*. New York, Free Press, 2007.

Chapter 7

Burrough, Bryan and John Helyar. *Barbarians at the Gate*. New York: Arrow Books, 1990.

Lewis, Michael. *Liar's Poker*. New York: W.W. Norton, 1989.

Stewart, James B. *Den of Thieves*. Riverside, New Jersey: Simon & Schuster, 1991.

Chapter 9

Chandler, Marc. *Making Sense of the Dollar—Exposing Dangerous Myths about Trade and Foreign Exchange*. New York: Bloomberg, 2009.

Chapter 10

Krugman, Paul. *The Return of Depression Economics*. New York: Norton, 2009.

Chapter 11

Mayer, Martin. *The Fed—The Inside Story of How the World's Most Powerful Financial Institution Drives the Markets*. New York: Free Press, 2001.

Wallison, Peter J. and Bert Ely. *Nationalizing Mortgage Risk: The Growth of Fannie Mae and Freddie Mac*. Washington, DC: AEI Press, 2000.

Chapter 12

Lowenstein, Roger. *When Genius Failed—The Rise and Fall of Long-Term Capital Management*. Maryland: Random House, 2000.

Chapter 13

Shiller, Robert J. *Irrational Exuberance*. Princeton, NJ: Broadway Business, 2006.

Chapter 14

Goldman Sachs Economics Group. The World and The Brics Dream. New York: The Goldman Sachs Group Inc., 2006.

Chapter 15

Yergin, Daniel. The Prize: The Epic Quest for Oil, Money and Power. New York: Free Press, 2008.

Chapter 16

Morris, Charles R. *The Two Trillion Dollar Meltdown: Easy Money, High Rollers and the Great Credit Crash*. New York: Public Affairs, 2009.

Tett, Gillian. *Fool's Gold—How the Bold Dream of a Small Tribe at J.P. Morgan Was Corrupted by Wall Street Greed and Unleashed a Catastrophe*. New York: Free Press, 2009.

Zuckerman, Gregory. *The Greatest Trade Ever—The Behind-the-Scenes Story of how John Paulson Defied Wall Street and Made Financial History.* New York: Broadway Business, 2009.

Chapter 17

Barbera, Robert J. *The Cost of Capitalism—Understanding Market Mayhem and Stabilizing Our Economic Future.* New York: McGraw Hill, 2009.

Minsky, Hyman. *John Maynard Keynes.* New York: McGraw Hill, 2008.

Chapter 18

Bookstaber, Richard. *A Demon of Our Own Design—Markets, Hedge Funds and the Perils of Financial Innovation.* New York: John Wiley & Sons, 2007.

Lo, Andrew. *Hedge Funds: An Analytic Perspective (Advances in Financial Engineering).* Princeton, NJ: Princeton University Press, 2008.

Chapter 19

Gorton, Gary B. *Slapped By The Invisible Hand—The Panic of 2007.* New York: Oxford University Press, 2010.

Wessel, David. *In Fed We Trust—Ben Bernanke's War on the Great Panic.* New York: Crown Business, 2009.

Chapter 20

Brummer, Alex. *The Crunch: Uncovering the Truth Behind the Great Credit Scandal.* London: Random House UK, 2008.

Kelly, Kate. *Street Fighters—The Last 72 Hours of Bear Stearns, the Toughest Firm on Wall Street.* New York: Portfolio, 2009.

Milne, Alistair. *The Fall of the House of Credit—What Went Wrong in Banking and What Can Be Done to Repair the Damage?* New York: Cambridge University Press, 2009.

Peston, Robert. *Who Runs Britain...and who's to blame for the economic mess we're in.* London: Hodder, 2008.

Chapter 21

Dumas, Charles. *China and America—A Time of Reckoning.* London: Profile Books, 2008.

Soros, George. *The New Paradigm for Financial Markets—The Credit Crisis of 2008 and What it Means.* New York: Public Affairs, 2008.

Chapter 22

Gasparino, Charles. *The Sellout—How Three Decades of Wall Street Greed and Government Mismanagement Destroyed the Global Financial System.* New York: Harper Business, 2009.

Sorkin, Andrew Ross. *Too Big To Fail—The inside story of how Wall Street and Washington fought to save the financial system – and themselves.* New York: Viking, 2009.

Chapter 24

Arnott, Robert, et al. *The Fundamental Index: A Better Way to Invest.* New York: Wiley, 2008.

Dimson, Elroy, Paul Marsh, and Mike Staunton. *Triumph of the Optimists: 101 Years of Global Investment Returns.* Princeton, NJ: Princeton University Press, 2002.

El-Erian, Mohamed. *When Markets Collide: Investment Strategies for the Age of Global Change*. New York: McGraw Hill, 2008.

Siegel, Jeremy. *Stocks for the Long Run: The Definitive Guide to Financial Market Returns and Long Term Investment Strategies*. 4th ed. New York: McGraw Hill, 2007.

Chapter 27

Bruner, Robert F. and Sean D Carr. *The Panic of 1907—Lessons Learned from the Market's Perfect Storm*. New York: Wiley, 2007.

Napier, Russell. *Anatomy of the Bear—Lessons from Wall Street's Four Great Bottoms* Hong Kong: CLSA Books, 2005.

Conclusion

Thaler, Richard H. and Cass R. Sunstein. *Nudge—Improving Decisions About Health, Wealth and Happiness*. New York: Penguin, 2009.

Index

W

X-Y-Z

FINANCIAL TIMES

In an increasingly competitive world, it is quality
of thinking that gives an edge—an idea that opens new
doors, a technique that solves a problem, or an insight
that simply helps make sense of it all.

We work with leading authors in the various arenas
of business and finance to bring cutting-edge thinking
and best-learning practices to a global market.

It is our goal to create world-class print publications
and electronic products that give readers
knowledge and understanding that can then be
applied, whether studying or at work.

To find out more about our business
products, you can visit us at www.ftpress.com.